BERTRAND RUSSELL

SPEAKS HIS MIND

BERTRAND RUSSELL SPEAKS HIS MIND

THE WORLD PUBLISHING COMPANY

CLEVELAND AND NEW YORK

Published by The World Publishing Company
2231 West 110th Street, Cleveland 2, Ohio

Published simultaneously in Canada by
Nelson, Foster & Scott Ltd.

Library of Congress Catalog Card Number: 60-6689

FIRST EDITION

This is a transcript of a Television Series filmed and produced
in England by VanCon Productions and distributed
by Telemat Sales Limited.

HC460

Contents

PUBLISHER'S NOTE

The following thirteen dialogues with Bertrand Russell were filmed for television during four and one-half days in the spring of 1959. No prepared script was used and no retakes were made, since Lord Russell insisted he was not an actor. His words were recorded on film—and in the pages of this book—as he first spoke them.

Woodrow Wyatt, the interviewer throughout the entire series, has had considerable experience with the B.B.C. as a television commentator. He is currently a member of Parliament for the Labour Party.

I.

What Is Philosophy?

I.

Lord Russell, what is philosophy?

LORD RUSSELL

Well, that's a very controversial question. I think no two philosophers will give you the same answer. My own view would be that philosophy consists of speculations about matters where exact knowledge is not yet possible. That would only be my answer—not anybody else's.

WYATT

What's the difference between philosophy and science?

RUSSELL

Well, roughly, you'd say science is what we know and philosophy is what we don't know. That's a simple definition and for that reason questions are perpetually passing over from philosophy into science as knowledge advances.

WYATT

Then when something is established and discovered it ceases to be philosophy and becomes science?

RUSSELL

Yes, and all sorts of questions that used to be labelled philosophy are no longer so labelled.

WYATT

What good is philosophy?

RUSSELL

I think philosophy has two uses really. One of them is to keep alive speculation about things that are not yet amenable to scientific knowledge; after all, scientific knowledge covers a very small part of the things that interest mankind and ought to interest them. There are a great many things of immense interest about which science, at present at any rate, knows little and I don't want people's imaginations to be limited and enclosed within what can be now known. I think that to enlarge your imaginative view of the world in the hypothetical realm is one of the uses of philosophy. But there's another use that I think is equally important, which is to show that there are things which we thought we knew and don't know. On the one hand, philosophy is to keep us thinking about things that we may come to know, and on the other hand to keep us modestly aware of how much that seems like knowledge isn't knowledge.

WYATT

Could you give us some illustrations of the sort of subjects which have been speculated about and then have produced some material results later?

RUSSELL

Yes. It's quite easy to do, especially from Greek philosophy. The Greeks invented a whole lot of hypotheses which turned out valuable later, but which in their day couldn't be tested. Take, for example, the atomic hypothesis. Democritus invented the atomic hypothesis that matter consists of little atoms, and after two thousand years and rather more than that, it turned out that this was the right scientific view, but in his day it was merely a suggestion. Or, again, take Aristarchus. Aristarchus was the first person who suggested that the earth went round the sun, and not the sun round the earth, and that the apparent revolution of the heavens every day was due to the earth rotating. That remained an almost buried and forgotten hypothesis until the time of Copernicus two thousand years later. But Copernicus would probably never have thought of it if it hadn't been for Aristarchus.

WYATT

How is this done—by some sort of intuition?

RUSSELL

Oh, no. The people who first think of these hypotheses can't say, "this is the truth"—they can only say, "this may be the truth." And if you have a good scientific imagination you can think of all sorts of things that might be true, and that's the essence of science. You first think of something that might be true—then you look to see if it is, and generally it isn't.

WYATT

But didn't Plato think that Democritus' theory about atoms was a lot of nonsense?

RUSSELL

Plato was horrified by him—said all his books ought to be burnt—because Plato didn't like science. He liked mathematics, but he didn't like anything else that was scientific.

WYATT

Now in this way philosophy, in a sense, becomes a kind of servant of science.

13

RUSSELL

Well, that's part of it, but of course it isn't only a servant of science—because there are a number of things that science can't deal with. All questions of values, for example. Science won't tell you what is good and what is bad—what is good or bad as an end, not just as a means.

WYATT

But what change has there been over the years in the attitude of philosophers and the public to philosophy would you say?

RUSSELL

Well, that depends upon the school of philosophy that you're thinking of. In both Plato and Aristotle the main thing was an attempt to understand the world, and that, I should say personally, is what philosophy ought to be doing. Then you come on to the Stoics and their emphasis was mainly on morality—that you ought to be stoical, you ought to endure misfortunes patiently—and that came to be a popular use of "philosopher."

WYATT

Would you say that Marx was a philosopher?

RUSSELL

Well, he was certainly in a sense a philosopher, but now there you have an important division amongst philosophers. There are some philosophers who exist to uphold the status quo, and others who exist to upset it—Marx of course belongs to the second lot. For my part I should reject both those as not being the true business of a philosopher, and I should say the business of a philosopher is not to change the world but to understand it, which is the exact opposite to what Marx said.

What kind of philosopher would you say you are?

Well, the only label I've ever given myself is logical atomist, but I'm not very keen on the label. I've rather avoided labels.

What does that mean? A logical atomist.

It means, in my mind, that the way to get at the nature of any subject matter you're looking at is analysis—and that you can analyze until you get to things that can't be analyzed any further and those would be logical atoms. I call them logical atoms because they're not little bits of matter. They're the ideas, so to speak, out of which a thing is built.

What is the main trend of philosophy today?

Well, one would have to distinguish there between English-speaking countries and continental European countries. The trends are much more separate than they used to be. Very much more. In English-speaking countries and especially in England, there is a new philosophy which has arisen, I think, through the desire to find a separate field for philosophy. In what I was saying a moment ago, it would appear that philosophy is merely incomplete science, and there are people who don't like that view. They want philosophy to have a sphere to itself. That had led into what you may call linguistic philosophy, in which the important thing for the philosopher is not to answer questions but to get the meaning of the questions quite clear. I myself can't agree to that view, but I can give you an illustration. I was once bicycling to Winchester, and I lost my way, and I went to a village shop and said, "Can you tell me the shortest way to Winchester?" and the man I asked called to a man in a back room and whom I couldn't see—"Gentleman wants to know the shortest way to Winchester." And a voice came back, "Winchester?"—"Aye"—"Way to Winchester?" —"Aye"—"Shortest way?"—"Aye"—"Don't know." And so I had to go on without getting any answer. Well, that is what Oxford philosophy thinks one should do.

WYATT

You mean get the question right, never mind about the answer?

RUSSELL

Yes. It's somebody else's business to give the answer.

WYATT

How does that differ from the continental approach now?

RUSSELL

The continental approach is—well—it's more full-blooded. I don't agree with it any more. But in a sense it's much more full-blooded and much more like the philosophies of earlier times. There are various kinds of philosophy that come from Kierkegaard's regard for existentialism, and

16

then there are philosophies designed to provide polemics for traditional religion. There are various things of that sort. I don't think myself that there's anything very important in all that.

WYATT

No, but what practical use is your sort of philosophy to a man who wants to know how to conduct himself?

RUSSELL

A great many people write to me saying they are now completely puzzled as to how they ought to conduct themselves, because they have ceased to accept the traditional signposts to right action and don't know what others to adopt. I think that the sort of philosophy I believe in is useful in this way: that it enables people to act with vigour when they are not absolutely certain that that is the right action. I think nobody should be certain of anything. If you're certain, you're certainly wrong, because nothing deserves certainty, and so one ought always to hold all one's beliefs with a certain element of doubt and one ought to be able to act vigorously in spite of the doubt. After all, this is what a general does when he is planning a battle. He doesn't quite know what the enemy will do, but if he's a good general he guesses right. If he's a bad general he guesses wrong. But in practical life one has to act upon probabilities, and what I should look to philosophy to do is to encourage people to act with vigour without complete certainty.

WYATT

Yes, but now how about this business of making people so uncertain about things they sort of believe and have faith in? Doesn't that rather disturb them?

RUSSELL

Well, it does for the time of course, and I think a certain amount of disturbance is an essential part of mental training, but if they have any knowledge of science they get the ballast which enables them to avoid being completely upset by the doubts that they ought to feel.

WYATT

What do you think is the future of philosophy?

RUSSELL

I don't think philosophy can, in future, have anything like the importance that it had either to the Greeks or in the Middle Ages. I think the rise of science inevitably diminishes the importance of philosophy.

WYATT

And it is possible that we've too many philosophers?

RUSSELL

Oh, well, I don't think a philosopher ought to express himself on that subject. I think people who are not philosophers should give their opinion of that.

WYATT

How would you summarize the value of philosophy in the present world and in the years to come?

RUSSELL

Well, I think it's very important in the present world. First, because, as I say, it keeps you realizing that there are very big and very important questions that science, at any rate at present, can't deal with and that a scientific attitude by itself is not adequate. And the second thing it does is to make people a little more modest intellectually and aware that a great many things which have been thought certain turned out to be untrue, and that there's no short cut to knowledge. And that the understanding of the world, which to my mind is the underlying purpose that every philosopher should have, is a very long and difficult business about which we ought not to be dogmatic.

2.

Religion

WOODROW WYATT

Have you ever had religious impulses, Lord Russell?

LORD RUSSELL

Oh, yes. When I was adolescent I was deeply religious. I was more interested in religion than in anything else, except perhaps mathematics. And being interested in religion led me—which it doesn't seem often to do—to look into the question of whether there was reason to believe it. I took up three questions. It seemed to me that God and immortality and free will were the three most essential questions, and I examined these one by one in the reverse order, beginning with free will, and gradually I came to the conclusion that there was no reason to believe in any of these. I thought I was going to be very disappointed, but oddly enough I wasn't.

WYATT

How did you come to convince yourself that there was no reason to believe in any of these three things?

RUSSELL

For free will, I think the argument was not a valid one, and I don't any longer think it's still conclusive. But I thought that because all the motions of matter are determined by the laws of dynamics, the motion of a man's lips when he speaks must be so determined, so that he can have no control over what he's going to say. I don't think that was a valid argument, but it convinced me at the time. About immortality—well, it seemed to me quite clear that the relation of body and mind, whatever it may be, is much more intimate than is commonly supposed, and that there's no reason to think that a mind persists when a brain decays. And as for God—well, there are a great many arguments that have been advanced in favour of the existence of God, and I thought, and I still think, that one and all they're invalid, and that nobody would have accepted such arguments if they hadn't wanted to believe the conclusions.

WYATT

I don't understand what you mean about laws of dynamics establishing that there was not such a thing as free will.

RUSSELL

Well, I have to explain that that was what I thought when I was adolescent. I thought then that, owing to the laws of dynamics, all the movements of matter, from the primitive nebula right onward were wholly determinate, and this involved any speaking. And therefore I thought that the laws of dynamics made it certain at the time of the primitive nebula exactly what Mr. A would say on every given occasion. Therefore Mr. A hadn't any free will as to what he would say.

WYATT

Do you think it is certain that there's no such thing as God, or simply that it is just not proved?

RUSSELL

I don't think it's certain that there is no such thing—no— I think that it is on exactly the same level as the Olympic gods, or Norwegian gods; they also may exist, the gods of Olympus and Valhalla. I can't prove they don't, but I think the Christian God has no more likelihood than they had. I think they are a bare possibility.

WYATT

Do you think that religion is good or harmful in its effects?

RUSSELL

I think most of its effects in history have been harmful. Religion caused the Egyptian priests to fix the calendar, and to note the occurrence of eclipses so well that in time they were able to predict them. I think those were beneficial effects of religion; but I think a great majority have been bad. I think they have been bad because it was held important that people should believe something for which there did not exist good evidence and that falsified everybody's thinking, falsified systems of education, and set up also, I think, complete moral heresy; namely, that it is right to believe certain things, and wrong to believe certain others, apart from the question of whether the things in question are true or false. In the main, I think religion has done a great deal of harm. Largely by sanctifying conservatism and adhesion to ancient habits, and still more by sanctifying intolerance and hatred. The amount of intolerance that has gone into religion, especially in Europe, is quite terrible.

WYATT

Do you mean that there is a kind of censorship of thought that prevents free thinking?

RUSSELL

I do—yes. I mean, if you take practically any school in the world—any school for boys and girls—you will find that a certain kind of belief is taught. It's one sort in Christian countries and another in Communist countries. But in both something is taught, and the evidence for what is taught is not impartially examined and the children are not encouraged to find out what there is to say on the other side.

WYATT

What is it that's made man, over the centuries, demand religion?

RUSSELL

I think mainly fear. Man feels himself rather powerless. There are three things that cause him fear. One is what Nature can do to him. It can strike him by lightning or swallow him up in an earthquake. And one is what other men can do—they can kill him in war. And the third, which has a great deal to do with religion, is what his own violent passions may lead him to do—things which he knows in a calm moment he would regret having done. For that reason most people have a great deal of fear in their lives, and religion helps them to be not so frightened by these fears.

WYATT

But that's not what the founders of religion themselves have always prescribed.

26

RUSSELL

No, but the founders of religions—I say relig
plural—have very little to do with what the...
teach. Very little indeed. Let's take an illustration. I have
found military men think that Christian belief is very
important in the contest with Eastern powers, and they
think that if you're not a Christian you won't be so vigorous about it. Well, I read the Sermon on the Mount over
again and I couldn't find a word in it to encourage the
H-bomb—not a word.

WYATT

Yes, but then do you think that religion is still doing harm
today? I mean, much of what you are criticizing happened
a long time ago. What about today?

RUSSELL

It's just the same today. Now this illustration that I gave
you about H-bombs is certainly not antiquated, yet I wish
it were, and I think that at this present day religion, as
embodied in the Churches, discourages honest thinking, in
the main, and gives importance to things that are not very
important. Its sense of importance seems to be quite wrong.

WYATT

Can you give an illustration of that?

RUSSELL

Yes, certainly. When the Roman Empire was falling, the
Fathers of the Church didn't bother much with the fall of
the Roman Empire. What they bothered with was how to

preserve virginity. That was what they thought important.

What did they do about that then?

They exhorted people and did not bother about seeing that the armies held the frontiers, or that the taxation system was reformed; they thought that far more important than having an empire. So in the present day when the human race is falling, I find that eminent divines think that it's much more important to prevent artificial insemination than it is to prevent the kind of world war that will exterminate the whole lot of us. That seems to me to show a lack of sense of proportion.

Yes, but wouldn't you agree that religions have sometimes done a lot of good in, say, spreading education, where perhaps no other system has been available, as in Burma, for instance, where the Buddhist monks have done a tremendous job educating the poor.

Well, I think it's possible, yes. I think the Benedictines did a certain amount of good in that way, but only after doing the harm. They first did a great deal of harm and then a little good.

But what about people who feel they must have a faith or a religion, or they can't face life at all?

RUSSELL

I say people who feel that are showing a kind of cowardice, which in any other sphere would be considered contemptible. But when it's in the religious sphere it's thought admirable, and I can't admire cowardice whatever sphere it's in.

WYATT

But why do you say it's cowardice?

RUSSELL

To say you can't face life without this or that. Everybody ought to be able to face life with whatever life offers them. It's a part of . . . of courage.

WYATT

But do you think that it's cowardice in the sense that people shovel their problems off onto God, or on a priest, say, or an organized religion, and then don't face these problems themselves?

RUSSELL

Yes. Now take the whole question of the very dangerous condition the world is in. I get letters constantly from people saying, "Oh, God will look after it." But He never has in the past, I don't know why they think He will in the future.

WYATT

You mean you think this is a very unwise doctrine to follow? It ought to be self-help rather than dependence upon somebody else to do it for you?

RUSSELL

Certainly. Yes.

WYATT

But then, if a religion is harmful, and yet man has always insisted on having one, what is the answer?

RUSSELL

Oh, man hasn't. Some men have, and those are the men who are used to it. In some countries, for instance, people walk on stilts, and they don't like walking without stilts. Religion is just the same thing. Some countries have got accustomed to it. But now I spent a year in China, and I found that the ordinary average Chinese had no religion whatsoever, and they were just as happy—I think, given their bad circumstances, happier than most Christians would have been.

WYATT

But I think a Christian would say that if he could convert them into being Christians they'd be much happier.

RUSSELL

Well, I don't think that's borne out by the evidence at all.

WYATT

Yes, but now doesn't man rather search for some cause of faith outside himself, which appears to be bigger than himself, not merely as a question of cowardice or leaning on it, but also wanting to do something for it?

30

RUSSELL

Well, but there are plenty of things bigger than oneself. I mean, first of all there's your family; then there's your nation; then there's mankind in general. Those are all bigger than oneself, and are quite sufficient to occupy any genuine feelings of benevolence that a man may have.

WYATT

Do you think that organized religion is always going to go on having the same sort of grip on mankind?

RUSSELL

I think it depends upon whether people solve their social problems or not. I think that if there go on being great wars and great oppressions and many people leading very unhappy lives, probably religion will go on, because I've observed that the belief in the goodness of God is inversely proportional to the evidence. When there's no evidence for it at all, people believe it, and when things are going well and you might believe it, they don't. So I think that if people solve their social problems religion will die out. But on the other hand, if they don't, I don't think it will. Now you can get illustrations of that in the past. In the eighteenth century when things were quiet, a great many educated people were freethinkers. Well, then came the French Revolution and certain English aristocrats came to the conclusion that free thought led to the guillotine, and so they dropped it, and they all became deeply religious and you got Victorianism. And the same thing again happened with the Russian Revolution. The Russian Revolution terrified people, and they thought that unless they believed in God their property would be confiscated, so they believed in Him. I think you'll find these social upheavals are very good for religion.

WYATT

Do you think that you and I are going to be completely snuffed out when we die?

RUSSELL

Certainly, yes. I don't see why not. I know that the body disintegrates, and I think that there's no reason whatever to suppose that the mind goes on when the body has disintegrated.

3.
War and Pacifism

3.

WOODROW WYATT

Lord Russell, do you think it reasonable to say there have been just wars.

LORD RUSSELL

Yes, I think it's quite reasonable, though of course you have to define what you mean by "just." You could mean, on the one hand, wars which have a good legal justification, and certainly there have been quite a number of wars where one side had a very good legal justification. Or you could mean wars which are likely to do good rather than harm, and that isn't at all the same classification. Not at all.

WYATT

Can you give examples of both sorts?

RUSSELL

Yes, easily enough. I think any resistance to aggression or invasion is just. The English were entirely just in resisting the Spanish Armada. I think the Hungarians were entirely just in their attempt to get liberty. One case fortunate, the other case unfortunate. But if you're going to take the question of issue then you get rather a different classification. You have to think whether good will come of it. Now take a war that had no justification whatsoever in the legal sense;

35

that is, the occupation of the North American continent by white men. I should say that on the whole that was a good thing, although it had no legal justification.

WYATT

What about the American War of Independence?

RUSSELL

Well, that I think was entirely justified. It was not, I suppose, legally justified and in actual fact if you want to go to America now, you have to make a statement which implies that you condemn George Washington. You have to say that you think no legally established government should be resisted by force or violence, but of course that is in retrospect.

WYATT

Now, do you think there have been successful wars on a long-term basis?

RUSSELL

Oh, yes, yes. Now take, to go back into ancient history, Alexander and Caesar. They were both great conquerors, they both engaged in wars which hadn't a legal justification, but I think the conquests that both of them made did good. Alexander's conquests established Hellenism throughout the Near East, spread the knowledge of the Greek language, and preserved for us the cultural heritage of Greece. I think it's very likely that none of us would know to this day what the Greeks did to civilization if it hadn't been for Alexander.

WYATT

What about Caesar?

RUSSELL

Well, Caesar conquered Gaul and made Gaul a part of the civilized world and incidently produced the French language which we all so much admire—which wouldn't have existed but for Caesar.

WYATT

What would you say the main causes of war are? Is it economics or is it the lunacy of rulers? Or is it outburst of popular enthusiasm or spirit?

RUSSELL

Well, there are examples of all of them. Sometimes one, sometimes another. Now take Frederick the Great's attack on Maria Theresa; that was, I think, solely the prerogative of a monarch. I don't think there was any other cause at all. In the eighteenth century it was quite apt to happen that monarchs went to war without any justification just for their own honour and glory. But since the eighteenth century that's not been so common.

WYATT

Apparently the "lunacy of rulers" category.

RUSSELL

Yes. Well, then you come to economic causes. Of course they were very operative in the long, long contest that England had with Spain. On our side the causes were mainly economic, on the Spanish side they were religious. The English fought for what was desirable and the Spaniards for what was undesirable; but that was a long business, which on our side was purely or almost purely

37

economic. Then, as for mob hysteria, well, that also plays a part. Walpole was Prime Minister for a very long time and was brought down at last by mob hysteria and the determination to go to war with Spain. We got the habit of going to war with Spain; we liked it and he didn't.

WYATT

You were a pacifist in the First World War. Don't you think you were a bit inconsistent in not being a pacifist in the Second World War?

RUSSELL

Well, I can't think so at all. I'd never have taken the view that all wars were just or that all wars were unjust. Never. I felt some were justified and some were not and I thought the Second World War was justified, but the First I thought was not.

WYATT

Why did you think the Second World War was justified?

RUSSELL

Because I thought Hitler was utterly intolerable. The whole Nazi outlook was absolutely dreadful, and I thought that if the Nazis conquered the world, as they obviously intended to do if they could, the world would become a place where life would be absolute hell and I thought we must stop this. We must.

WYATT

Do you think still that it was a mistake to have fought the First World War?

RUSSELL

Yes, I think England should have been neutral. I said so at the time and I still stick to that. I think if we had remained neutral in the First World War it would have been rather a short war; it would have ended with Germany a good deal more powerful than it was at the beginning, but not all-powerful by any means, and the Germany of the Kaiser, in spite of the propaganda that existed in England at that time, was not so very bad. In fact there are very few governments at the present day that are as good as the Kaiser's government was—very few; because when you go to war against a bad government you always make it worse. I don't think that quite applies to the war against the Nazis because nothing could be worse. But it does generally apply and if we had remained neutral in 1914 we should not have had Nazis and we should not have had the Communists. The Communists quite obviously resulted from the disintegration of the Russian army and the general complete chaos in Russia at that time, which wouldn't have happened if the war had been short.

WYATT

What would have happened in Russia?

RUSSELL

In Russia you would have had a revolution on the lines that the 1905 revolution was intended to be. Almost certainly the social revolutionaries would have come into power, and they were nothing like so bad as the Communists. I think they would have achieved a quite tolerable state of affairs.

WYATT

Do you think that in Germany there wouldn't have been anything like Nazis and that it would have gradually progressed to a reasonable sort of democracy?

RUSSELL

Yes, it was already doing so. It was doing so at quite a reasonable pace, quite as fast as we ever did it in England at an earlier time. I think Germany would have become a reasonable parliamentary democracy in time and certainly would not have developed that Nazi philosophy which was a reaction to ruin.

WYATT

But supposing we hadn't fought the First World War. Surely the Germans would have overrun France, and having done that, looked around at England and said, "Well, let's polish that off."

RUSSELL

I don't think there's any reason to think so. What the Germans wanted were certain quite limited things. They wanted to be allowed to have a good navy, they wanted to be allowed more colonial expansion than we quite liked, and they wanted a certain domination in the Balkans—they actually wanted Austria to have a certain domination in the Balkans. But the Kaiser's aims, as far as I can see, were quite finite and limited. I don't think he was out for world domination.

WYATT

But on the other hand, from the British point of view the First World War was a just war, wasn't it?

RUSSELL

Oh, yes, it was legally just, if you take it that we went to war in defence of Belgium, which is of course a moot point; but if you agree to that, then it was certainly legally just. But I don't think that every war which has a legal justification ought to be fought.

WYATT

Do you think that people enjoy wars?

RUSSELL

Well, a great many do. It was one of the things that struck me in 1914 when the First War began. All my pacifist friends, with whom I was in time to work, thought that wars are imposed upon populations by the wicked machinations of governments, but I walked about the streets of London and looked in people's faces, and I saw that they were really all happier than they were before the war had started. I said so in print and I caused great heart-searchings among my pacifist friends, who didn't like my saying this. I still think that a great many people enjoy a war provided it's not in their neighbourhood and not too bad; when the war comes onto your own territory it's not so pleasant.

WYATT

As so many people enjoy wars, what are they to do with their aggressive feelings if they're not allowed to have one?

RUSSELL

I think the feelings are not essentially aggressive, they're adventurous. And I think it's very, very important that

41

opportunities for adventure should as far as possible be open to all that part of the population that likes adventure. You ought to be able to climb mountains without spending a great deal of money on it. You ought to be able to go to the North Pole and the South Pole if you want to. You ought to have every kind of opportunity for adventure.

WYATT

Do you think the Scandinavians—or, say, the Swedes—are happier after not having had a war for so long?

RUSSELL

Oh, yes, they haven't had a war since 1814, and as far as I have seen Sweden, it's one of the happiest countries I know. I think they enjoy life thoroughly, and I have never noticed any sign that they have felt thwarted through not being in a war.

WYATT

A lot of them commit suicide.

RUSSELL

Oh, yes, they do that, but they do that because they're not restrained by religion. They're not a very religious population. Religious Swedes all went to the Middle West of America and the population that remained in Sweden was rather irreligious.

WYATT

But isn't it a part of human nature to have wars?

RUSSELL

Well, I don't know what human nature is supposed to be. But your nature is infinitely malleable, and that is what people don't realize. Now if you compare a domestic dog with a wild wolf you will see what training can do. The domestic dog is a nice comfortable creature, barks occasionally, and he may bite the postman, but on the whole he's all right; whereas the wolf is quite a different thing. Now you can do exactly the same thing with human beings. Human beings according to how they're treated will turn out totally different and I think the idea that you can't change human nature is so silly.

WYATT

But surely we've been a long time at the job of trying to persuade people not to have wars, and yet we haven't got very far.

RUSSELL

Well, we haven't tried to persuade them. A few, a very few, have tried to, but the great majority have not.

WYATT

Don't you think that the Swedes might be a bit happier if they had had a war to buck them up a bit?

RUSSELL

I don't think there's the least reason to suppose so. No. At present most people have had a war, and I think they're definitely not as happy as the Swedes are. At least that's my impression from travelling.

WYATT

Would you say people weren't quite so happy with the Second World War then?

RUSSELL

Well, the Second World War took a very different course from the First. In the First War, of course, people who had to fight in it were not at all happy because they knew they were very, very likely to be killed. It was the people who stayed at home who so enjoyed it. But in the Second War, well, it was a very, very different thing, and I think people were blasé—they'd had the emotion of war in the First World War.

WYATT

Earlier in this conversation you talked of a war against Spain, which was induced against the wishes of Prime Minister Walpole by mob hysteria. Do you think that we're less vulnerable to mob hysteria today?

RUSSELL

No, not less than in that time. I think that education, which leads people to be able to read, has through the press immensely increased mob hysteria. But there's a contrary tendency coming in now, mainly I think through television, because people get their news of the world now sitting at home and not sitting in excited halls of large crowds of people who begin to shout. And I think it's large assemblies such as you get in big public meetings that are the main cause of mob hysteria. Insofar as meetings count for less I think mob hysteria will grow less.

WYATT

Do you think that the sort of situation in which crowds assemble in Trafalgar Square when a war is about to be declared won't arise so readily now?

RUSSELL

Well, I suppose it will. Trafalgar Square, after all is very handy and it's easy to get there. I suppose Trafalgar Square will go on, but not to the same degree I think as it would otherwise. Of course I know it's very absurd when a war is imminent. Immense crowds assemble in Trafalgar Square to applaud. They echo the Government's decision to have them killed. It's odd. It's not what you would expect of this thing called human nature. That is how it works, but I think that will grow less.

4.

Communism and
Capitalism

4.

What do you think are the similarities between communism and capitalism, Lord Russell?

LORD RUSSELL

There are quite a lot of similarities which can result almost inevitably, I think, from modern technique. Modern technique requires very large organizations, centrally directed, and produces a certain executive type to run them. And that is equally true in communist and in capitalist countries, if they are industrially developed.

WYATT

Do you think that they produce a similar attitude of mind, these large organizations in, say, Russia and America?

RUSSELL

I think so, though not completely. I mean, there are differences in degree, but not in kind . . . I think there is a very great similarity between a really powerful American executive and a Soviet administrator. There are more limitations upon what the American executive can do, but in kind they're the same sort of thing.

WYATT

Do you think this leads to people in Russia and, say, America wanting the same sort of things as ideals in life: motor-cars, material rewards, and so on?

RUSSELL

I think it leads to that to a very great extent, yes. I mean, I think there's a great deal of humbug talked about Russians being materialistic. After all, most people are materialistic in the sense that the things they want are the things that money can buy. It's a normal part of human nature, and I don't think that there's nearly as much difference in the matter of materialism between East and West as propaganda has led us to suppose.

WYATT

After the First World War you went to Russia, and at a time when most people of the Left were giving three cheers for Russia, you struck rather a discordant note. Do you still think that what was going on in Russia then was undesirable?

RUSSELL

Oh, I do, and I think the Russian regime that has resulted in not particularly desirable from my point of view, because it doesn't allow for liberty, it doesn't allow for free discussion, it doesn't allow for the unfettered pursuit of knowledge. It encourages dogmatism, it encourages the use of force to spread opinion, it does a number of things which as an old Liberal I find very, very distasteful indeed.

WYATT

Do you think it is still doing these things?

RUSSELL

Oh, I think so. I think with a little less virulence than it had in Stalin's lifetime, but it still does them certainly.

WYATT

You've talked about the Communist regime in Russia preventing freedom of thought. How is it, then, that they've been able to make such remarkable advances in the scientific field?

RUSSELL

Well, I will confess that I was rather surprised that they were able to, but I don't think I ought to have been. We had the example of Japan. Japan, when it started westernizing, didn't westernize in thought, but only in technique, and until it was defeated in the Second World War it retained all the old Japanese beliefs, although it achieved a thoroughly modern technique. Now the Russians haven't retained the old beliefs, but they have got a creed which they enforce and which doesn't interfere with technique. They've discovered how to enable people to think about technical problems without thinking about anything higher.

WYATT

Do you think that the Communists in Russia have succeeded in making the Russians happier than they were?

RUSSELL

I really don't know. I think it's possible that they may now be happier. They certainly were not in Stalin's day. In Stalin's day I should think the average Russian was less happy than in the Czar's time, but I think perhaps now they are.

WYATT

WYATT

What did you think of Lenin when you met him?

RUSSELL

To tell you the truth, I was rather disappointed by Lenin. I admitted of course that he had some very great qualities; he had incredible courage, inflexible will, great determination, and was out to embody a creed, not out for himself. I don't think he was out for himself except insofar as he himself was necessary to his creed. He was an honest man in that sense. But I thought his creed was a narrow one, that he was a fanatic, that he was quite incapable of thinking outside the Marxist orbit.

WYATT

Was he a cruel man?

RUSSELL

Well, that was the impression that I got. I don't think he was as cruel as Stalin, but I think there were certainly elements of cruelty in him—yes.

WYATT

What do you think of the defects in the way in which the free world presents itself and conducts itself?

RUSSELL

Well, there are several defects, but the most important is that it's not free. It has no right to the title, "free world." You know, of course, we in England have all been very much aware of the McCarthy reign of terror that existed in America, but we don't, I think, quite realize that the same sort of thing happens here. That if you want to go into the Civil Service you're submitted to espionage, and not merely to being asked direct questions as to what your opinions are, but your university teachers and such are expected to act as government spies.

WYATT

Do you mean that when somebody who has just come down from Oxford applies for a job in government service his ex-tutor will be asked, "Do you think he is a reliable person from a political point of view?"

RUSSELL

That is happening. A great many have refused to answer such questions, but it is happening. I don't know whether in regard to people in Oxford, but it certainly is happening.

WYATT

But might that not be a reasonable precaution for a government to take so that they can avoid having people in their service who will go and give government secrets to foreign powers?

RUSSELL

I don't think so. I think all that business of spies and secrets and all the rest is very, very much overdone. As a matter of fact, the Russians are quite able to discover everything for themselves, and I don't think the spies and traitors really did us much harm or them much good. I think it's one of those things that are melodramatic and catch people's imagination.

WYATT

What else would you say was wrong with the way in which the free world presents itself?

RUSSELL

Well, again let's take another example of how they don't care for freedom. They are prepared to ally themselves with Franco, and I think Franco's regime has all the defects that the Communist regime has. If you're on any ideological basis you've no business to ally yourselves with people who are doing exactly the things that you say you object to.

WYATT

What would you call it if you wouldn't call it a free world?

RUSSELL

I should call it the capitalist world.

WYATT

Even though it includes countries like Sweden and Norway and Denmark which aren't really capitalist?

RUSSELL

Perhaps it wouldn't be fair to call it quite that. I think the real important distinction is parliamentary democracy. The Western world believes in parliamentary democracy, except in places like Spain and Portugal. But in general, for its own sake at home, it believes in it and the communist world doesn't. I think perhaps that's the most important difference.

WYATT

Apart from the things you've mentioned, what do you think is actually wrong with the communist doctrine?

RUSSELL

I think the most important thing that is wrong in communist doctrine is the belief in benevolent despotism. A belief which is really ancient and existed in all sorts of communities, but has always proved itself wrong, because when you take a benevolent man and make him a despot, his despotism survives but his benevolence rather fades away. The whole theory of communism is that you give an enormous amount of power to people who are adherents to a certain creed, and you hope that they will exercise that enormous power benevolently. Whereas it seems to me that everybody—with very few exceptions—misuses power, and therefore the important thing is to spread power as evenly as you can, and not give immense power to some small clique.

WYATT

Do you mean that the Communists in Russia, having got hold of this apparatus of government, now no longer believe in the dictatorship of the proletariat?

RUSSELL

Yes, I do. The proletariat is a Pickwickian word, as it's used in Russia. When I was there I found that Lenin counted as a proletarian, but the absolutely miserable beggars in the street who couldn't get enough to eat were counted lackeys of the bourgeoisie.

55

WYATT

I see what you mean. But to move on to another area where communism is practised on a very large scale—China—do you think that China is as great a threat to what I won't now call the free world, but the parliamentary, as Russia is?

RUSSELL

Yes, I should think in the long run, perhaps a greater threat. China is newer to it than the Russians are, and is still at an earlier and more fanatical stage than the Russians have reached. And China has a much larger population than Russia. It has a population which is naturally industrious—they have always been industrious; and it is capable of being a more powerful state than Russia and I think has at least as great men.

WYATT

Do you think the Russians think this about China?

RUSSELL

Well, you know one can't tell. They are very careful not to let you know, and if you give any hint of such a thing in a question, they are very, very cagey in their answers. But one would suppose that they must.

WYATT

I mean, do you think it is significant that they haven't given China the important secrets of how to make the atom- and H-bombs?

RUSSELL

Oh, yes, I think it is.

WYATT

Do you think that the tension between the communist and the noncommunist world is doing a great deal of harm to liberty generally?

RUSSELL

Oh, yes, it's doing immense harm to liberty. . . . Any state of tension like that inevitably does, and it prevents people from thinking clearly. You see, the police both in the East and the West think that if you studied the opposite system you would infallibly agree with it, and therefore we mustn't be allowed to know anything about it. And that . . . that is really absurd. That's one thing that it does. Another thing it does is to spread an atmosphere of suspicion, and people may be very unjustly suspected and completely ruined by it. I think the tension does enormous harm.

WYATT

But how can you expect the Russians to allow their people freely to study the workings of the parliamentary world when it's highly likely that they might like the look of unfettered thought better than the system they live under?

RUSSELL

Well, it would have to be a reciprocal thing. You see, in America certainly, very serious obstacles are put in your way if you want to study the Russian method. There would have to be reciprocal agreement that each should be allowed to study the other, and I think just as many Americans would like the Russian system as Russians would like the American one.

WYATT

But in Britain people study communism like mad.

RUSSELL

Well, certainly. There are a certain number of people who come to like it, and they're allowed to have university posts, which would be unthinkable in America.

WYATT

Do you think it is possible for communism and capitalism to learn to live side by side in the world together?

RUSSELL

Yes, it certainly is possible. It's only a question of getting used to each other. Now take the . . . the Christians and the Mohammedans. They fought each other for about six centuries, during which neither side got any advantage over the other, and at the end of that time some man of genius said: "Look, why shouldn't we stop fighting each other and make friends?" And they did, and that's all right, and just the same thing can happen with capitalism and communism as soon as each side realizes that it can't gain the world.

WYATT

But how are they going to come to this realization?

RUSSELL

Oh, by experience. Of course, we can't wait six centuries because there won't be any of us left after six centuries of conflict such as the Mohammedans and Christians had. But I think it's quite possible to get governments on both sides to realize that they should agree.

5.
Taboo Morality

5.

WOODROW WYATT

WOODROW WYATT

Lord Russell, what do you mean by taboo morality?

LORD RUSSELL

Well, I mean the sort of morality that consists in giving a set of rules mainly as to things you must not do, without giving any reasons for those rules. Sometimes reasons cannot be found, other times they can, but in any case the rules are considered absolute and these things you must not do.

WYATT

What sort of things?

RUSSELL

Well, now, it depends on the level of civilization. Taboo morality is characteristic of the primitive mind. It is the only kind, I think, in primitive tribes where, for example, it would be a rule you must not eat out of one of the chief's dishes. If you did you'd probably die, so they say, and there are all sorts of rules of that sort. I remember the King of Dahomey had a rule that he must not look long in any one direction because if he did, there would be tempests in that part of his dominions, and so there was a rule that he must always be looking round.

61

WYATT

Well, those are the sorts of taboos from what we would, I suppose, consider primitive societies. What about our own?

RUSSELL

Well, our own morality is just as full of taboos. There are all sorts, even in the most august things. Now there is one sin definitely recognized to be a sin, which I've never committed. It says, "Thou shalt not covet thy neighbor's ox." Now I never have.

WYATT

Yes, but what about more matter-of-fact everyday rules than that? Are there examples of taboo morality you can give us?

RUSSELL

Oh, yes. Of course a great deal of taboo morality is entirely compatible with what one might call rational morality. For instance, that you shouldn't steal or that you shouldn't murder. Those are precepts which are entirely in accord with reason, but they are set forth as taboos; they have consequences that they ought not to have. For instance, in the case of murder it is considered that it forbids euthanasia, which I think a rational person would be in favour of.

WYATT

Do you put into the category of taboo morality things like Hindus saying you shouldn't eat beef?

RUSSELL

Yes, it is typical of Hindu morality that Hindus shouldn't eat beef. The Mohammedans and the Jews say you mustn't eat pork, and there is no reason for that, it's just taboo.

WYATT

Well, you don't think these taboos serve any useful purpose?

RUSSELL

Some do and some don't, it all depends. I mean, if you get a rational basis for your ethic you can then look into the taboos and see which are useful, but the prohibition of beef, I should say, doesn't do any good at all.

WYATT

Well, if you don't believe in religion, and you don't, and if you don't think much of the unthinking rules of taboo morality, do you believe in any general system of ethics?

RUSSELL

Yes, but it's very difficult to separate ethics altogether from politics. Ethics, it seems to me, arise in this way. A man is inclined to do something which benefits him and harms his neighbours. Well, if it harms a good many of his neighbours they will combine together and say, "Look, we don't like this sort of thing, we will see to it that it doesn't benefit the man," and that leads to the criminal law, which is perfectly rational. It's a method of harmonizing the general and private interest.

WYATT

But now isn't it thought rather inconvenient if everybody goes about with his own kind of private system of ethics instead of accepting a general one?

RUSSELL

It would be if that were so, but in fact they're not so private as all that because, as I was saying a moment ago, they get embodied in the criminal law and, apart from the criminal law, in public approval and disapproval. People don't like to incur public disapproval and in that way the accepted code of morality becomes a very potent thing.

WYATT

Is there such a thing as sin?

RUSSELL

No. I think sin is difficult to define. If you mean merely undesirable actions, of course there are undesirable actions. When I say "undesirable" I mean that they are actions which I suppose do more harm than good, and of course there are. But I don't think sin is a useful conception. I think sin is something that it is positively good to punish, such as murder, not only because you want to prevent murder, but because the murderer deserves to suffer.

WYATT

Are you saying that the idea of sin is really an excuse for cruelty in many cases?

RUSSELL

I think very largely. I mean, I think only cruel people could have invented hell. People with humane feelings

64

would not have liked the thought that those who do things on earth which are condemned by the morality of their tribe will suffer eternally without any chance of amendment. I don't think decent people would have ever adopted that view.

WYATT

Then you mean the concept of sin is really a chance to get one's aggressive feelings out?

RUSSELL

Yes, I think so. It's the essence of what you might call a stern morality. It's to enable you to inflict suffering without a bad conscience, and therefore it is a bad thing.

WYATT

How are we to disapprove of things if we do not accept the proposition that there is such a thing as a sin?

RUSSELL

Well, the disapproval in itself combined with the criminal law does, I think, all that you can do. You have to have a certain kind of public opinion. Now you see how important that is if you read the histories of the Italian Renaissance— the sort of histories that produced the Machiavellian theories. Public opinion tolerated things then which, in most times, public opinion would not tolerate.

WYATT

Would you agree, though, that some things are wicked?

RUSSELL

I shouldn't like to use that word. I should say some things do more harm than good; and if you know that they're going to do more harm than good, well, you'd better not do them. If you like to use the word "wicked," you can, but I don't think it's a useful word.

WYATT

A large part of taboo morality affects sexual relations. And a very large part of your output in writing has been about sexual relations. What advice would you give now to people who want to conduct themselves sensibly so far as sex is concerned?

RUSSELL

Well, I should like to say, by way of preface, that only about one per cent of my writings are concerned with sex, but the conventional public is so obsessed with sex that it hasn't noticed the other ninety-nine per cent of my writings. I should like to say that to begin with, and I think one per cent is a reasonable proportion of human interest to assign to that subject. But I should deal with sexual morality exactly as I should with everything else. I should say that if what you're doing does no harm to anybody there's no reason to condemn it. And you shouldn't condemn it merely because some ancient taboo has said that this is wrong. You should look into whether it does any harm or not, and that's the basis of sexual morality as of all other.

WYATT

Would you say that rape is to be condemned, but that ordinary fornication, provided that it doesn't hurt anybody, isn't necessarily to be condemned?

RUSSELL

Yes, I should certainly say that rape is just like any other bodily violence. As for fornication, well, you'd have to look into the circumstances to see whether there was on this occasion a reason against it or whether there wasn't. But you shouldn't block condemnation always and under all circumstances.

WYATT

Do you think it's right to have rules about what can and can't be published?

RUSSELL

Well, that's a question on which I feel in rather an extreme position. A position which I'm afraid very few people agree with. I think there ought to be no rules whatever prohibiting improper publications. I think that partly because if there are rules stupid magistrates will condemn really valuable work because it happens to shock them. That's one of the reasons; another reason is that I think prohibitions immensely increase people's interest in pornography, as in anything else. I used often to go to America during Prohibition, and there was far more drunkenness than there was before, far more, and I think that prohibition of pornography has much the same effect. Now, I'll give you an illustration of what I mean about prohibitions. The philosopher Empedocles thought it was very very wicked to munch laurel leaves, and he laments that he will have to spend ten thousand years in outer darkness because he munched laurel leaves. Now nobody's ever told me not to munch laurel leaves and I've never done it, but Empedocles who was told not to, did it. And I think the same applies to pornography.

WYATT

Do you think that if everything that everybody wrote of an obscene nature were published, then it wouldn't increase people's interest at all?

RUSSELL

I think it would diminish it. Suppose, for instance, filthy post cards were permitted. I think for the first year or two there would be a great demand for them, and then people would get bored and nobody would look at them again.

WYATT

And this would apply to writing and so on as well?

RUSSELL

I think so, within the limits of what is sensible. I mean, if it was a fine piece of art, a fine piece of work, the people would read it, but not because it was pornographic.

WYATT

To come back to the basis of what we've just been talking about—the unthinking rules of taboo morality. What damage do you think they are doing now?

RUSSELL

Well, they do two different sorts of harm. One sort of harm is that they are usually ancient and come down from a different sort of society from that in which we live, where really a different ethic was appropriate, and very often they

68

are not appropriate to modern times. I think that applies in particular to artificial insemination, which is a thing that the moralists of the past hadn't thought of. That is one sort of harm. Another is that taboo moralities tend to perpetuate ancient cruelties. I can give several examples of that. Take, for instance, human sacrifice. The Greeks, at a very early period in their history, began to turn against human sacrifice, which they had practised, and they wanted to abolish it; but there was one institution which did not want it abolished, and stuck up for it, and that was the Oracle at Delphi. It made its living out of superstition, and it didn't want superstition diminished; so it stood up for human sacrifice long after other Greeks had given it up. That is one example. I can give you another example of some importance. It had always been held that to cut up a corpse was extraordinarily wicked; Vesalius, who was a very eminent doctor in the time of Emperor Charles V, realized that you couldn't really do a great many valuable medical things unless you dissected corpses, and he used to dissect them. Now Emperor Charles V was a valetudinarian, and as this was the only doctor who could keep him well, he protected him. But after the Emperor had abdicated, there was nobody to protect Vesalius, and he was condemned for having dissected a body which they said was not quite dead; as a penalty he had to go on a pilgrimage to the Holy Land. On the way he got shipwrecked and died of hardship and that was the end of him. All this because there was this taboo against cutting up corpses. Taboo morality certainly is doing harm today. Take, for example, the question of birth control. There is a very powerful taboo by certain sections of the community which is calculated to do very enormous harm. Very enormous harm. It is calculated to promote poverty and war and to make the solution of many social problems impossible. That is, I think, perhaps the most important, and I think there are a number of others. Indissolubility of marriage is definitely harmful; it is based solely upon ancient tradition and not upon examination of present circumstances.

6.

Power

6.

WOODROW WYATT

Lord Russell, what are the impulses that make men want power?

LORD RUSSELL

I should suppose that the original impulses, out of which subsequent power-loving people got their drive, came in times that were liable to occasional famine, and when you wanted to be sure that if the food supply ran short it wouldn't be you who would suffer. It required that you have power.

WYATT

What are the kinds of power that have developed since then?

RUSSELL

Well, there are different ways of classifying powers. One of the most obvious, I think, is that of direct power over the body. This is the power of armies and police forces. Then there is the power of reward and punishment, which is called the economic power. And then finally there is propaganda power, a power to persuade. I think these are the three main kinds of power.

WYATT

Lord Russell, would you say that there can be good as well as bad motives for wanting power?

RUSSELL

I should most certainly. I should say that almost everybody who has had any important effect in the world has been actuated by some form of love of power, and that applies to saints as well as sinners. It applies too, I think, to every energetic person.

WYATT

Doesn't it very often happen that the person who wants the good things also wants power because he's rather vain?

RUSSELL

Yes, it does very often happen, all because the sheer love of power outweighs the wish to get this or that done. That is why Lord Acton was quite right to say that power corrupts, because pleasure in the exercise of power is something that grows with experience of power. Take, for example, Cromwell. I have no doubt that Cromwell went into politics with entirely laudable motives because there were certain things he thought were extremely important to the country that he wanted to see done. But after he'd been in power for a certain length of time he just wanted power, and that is why on his deathbed he said that he was afraid he'd fallen from grace. Oh, certainly, yes. I think every person who shows much energy wants power. But I only want one sort of power. I want power over opinions.

74

WYATT

Do you think that the power you've had over opinions has corrupted you?

RUSSELL

Well, I don't know if it has. It's not for me to say that. I think other people will have to be the judge of that.

WYATT

Can we return to the three kinds of powers? Take physical power first. The power of authority—the police, the apparatus of governing—do you think that that needs curbing?

RUSSELL

Yes, one needs the possibility of pulling up the holders of immediate power if they do wrong. That was the idea of power of impeachment. You could hold up a man if he seemed to be doing wrong, and it's very important that that should exist. Very important.

WYATT

Now do you think it's gone too far though? That, at the moment, people don't have enough protection from arbitrary power and the police and so forth?

RUSSELL

Oh, I think it certainly is true, but it's not very easy to see what to do about it. In the modern world decisions have to be taken quickly. You must leave the capacity for decisions in the hands of a very few so that protection from

their power is not very easy. But it's a very important problem and one that ought to be considered.

WYATT

How would you deal with this?

RUSSELL

Well, it depends upon what departments of life you're
thinking of. I should say, for instance, that police power
has been proved in many modern states to be a very dangerous thing indeed. Wherever the Communists have been
trying to get hold of a state they hadn't previously domin-
ated, the first thing they try to get hold of is the manage-
ment of the police. Then they can settle who they can put in
jail and they can cook the evidence as to what is done, so
that I think the power of the police can be a very dangerous thing and has been proved so. Now I should like to see
everywhere two police forces, one to prove guilt and the
other to prove innocence.

WYATT

Wouldn't that rather complicate the issue and become very
expensive for the governments concerned?

RUSSELL

Well, certainly, I think it might. But suppose, for instance,
that you were unjustly accused of a murder. The taxpayer
pays all the expense of proving that you did the murder,
and you, out of your own pocket, have to prove—have to
pay the expense of proving—that you didn't, and that
seems hardly fair. It's better that ninety-nine guilty men
should escape than that one innocent man should be punished. But we conduct our affairs on the opposite princi-

ple—that it's more desirable that ninety-nine innocent men should be punished than that one guilty man should escape —because we think that the taxpayer should pay for the proof of the guilt and the private person should pay for the proof of the innocence.

WYATT

Yes, but it can't very often happen that somebody is wrongly convicted. Is it really worth while for the state to go to this enormous expense in order to establish every now and again that somebody may have been unjustly accused?

RUSSELL

We don't know how often it happens, that's part of the argument. It's not the sort of thing the police will be likely to disclose. For all we know it may happen very often. We really don't know, and in any case the enormous expense would not be more than the expense which is at present incurred in proving the evidence.

WYATT

Now let's move over a bit more to governmental actions. Do you think that governments ought not to have quite such freedom to decide issues quickly, without referring back to electorates and so on? And if so, wouldn't this make an awful lot of inefficiency in action?

RUSSELL

Well, yes, I think it might. And there are some places in the world that we live in now where it's impossible to refer things to a referendum or anything of this sort. Questions of peace and war, which are the most important of all, have to be decided quickly. It would require a very great change in the institutions of the whole world to make the decision of peace or war one which could be taken slowly and deliberated on again. It would be a very good thing if you could.

WYATT

But would you on the whole be in favour of a bit more inefficiency?

RUSSELL

I think certainly where bad actions are concerned the more inefficient the better. Such is human nature—or such has it been hitherto—that there are a great many bad actions which people are very anxious to perform efficiently. I think one might say that the human race has survived owing to inefficiency, but inefficiency is now diminishing, and therefore the human race is threatened with extinction.

WYATT

How have laziness and inefficiency helped man to survive?

RUSSELL

By diminishing their capacity to kill each other. If you are a clever murderer you're efficient and you murder a lot of people. If you're a stupid murderer you get caught and you're stopped. Unfortunately the murderers are getting cleverer and cleverer.

WYATT

Can we turn a moment to another form of power—economic. Do you think that Marx put too much emphasis on the importance of economic power?

RUSSELL

Marx, in the first place, put too much emphasis on economic as opposed to other forms of power. Second, misled by the state of business in the 1840's in England, he thought that it was ownership which gives power and not executive control. Both those interpretations led him to propose a panacea for all the ills of the world which proved entirely fallacious.

WYATT

How do you rate the importance of economic power?

RUSSELL

Oh, the importance of economic power is very great indeed, but it's only one form of power. I couldn't say that it was more important than military power or more important than propaganda power. Now let's take an illustration. You remember that Queen Boadicea rebelled against the Romans. She rebelled because Seneca had lent her a lot of money at a very high rate of interest and she couldn't find the money. Well, that was because Seneca had economic power at that time. But after Boadicea had been completely subdued by the Roman army, Seneca himself was sentenced to death by the Emperor, and that was not economic power, it was military power.

WYATT

Do you think economic power needs curbing?

RUSSELL

Yes, I think every kind of power needs curbing because certainly the power to starve large regions is very undesirable. I think the economic power of certain regions in the Middle East to withhold oil if they like is not at all a desirable kind of thing.

WYATT

Propaganda power—how important is that?

RUSSELL

Oh, propaganda power is enormously important, and it's importance has always been recognized. People say the blood of the martyrs is the seed of the church. That means that the blood of the martyrs has great propaganda power. People say great is truth and it will prevail, by which they mean that the opinion now currently held will prevail. Propaganda is enormously important in all sorts of ways. Certainly the Christian religion was established entirely without the help of either economic or military power.

WYATT

Do you think that propaganda power is always bad?

RUSSELL

Oh, certainly not. Oh, no. It's bad when it confuses bad opinions with good ones, but I certainly don't think it's always bad. You'd have to say that all education was bad if you said that, because all education consists of a kind of propaganda.

WYATT

Do you think that the strength of the power of propaganda needs curbing? Have people got into a state by being subjected to mass communications in which they can't think clearly for themselves?

RUSSELL

Oh, certainly propaganda needs enormous curbing. I understand that the opinions of the average Russian as to what takes place in Western countries are very, very far from the truth and that is due to the propaganda control over education which exists in communist countries. There is a slightly less tight control in noncommunist countries, but still a very great control aiming not to make people think truly, but to make them think what their government thinks.

WYATT

What about the West? Does the propaganda power need curbing much in the West?

RUSSELL

It certainly needs curbing. Not as much, but it does need curbing, because you will find that in what is taught in schools and in universities there is not a free and unfettered competition between different kinds of opinion, but certain opinions are very much favoured at the expense of others.

WYATT

Now how important is this whole problem of use and abuse of power in a man's life?

RUSSELL

I think it's of quite enormous importance, and in fact I think it's almost the main difference between a good government and a bad one. In a good government power is used with limitations and with checks and balances and in a bad government it's used indiscriminately. I think it's enormously important.

WYATT

Do you think that, broadly speaking, the democratic systems of the West produce a roughly reasonable balance between the need of government to take action in a firm and decisive way, and the need of the government to satisfy people that the action they're taking is in conformity with what people want?

RUSSELL

Well, certainly we are very much better than totalitarian governments. Very much better. For the reason that we have certain ultimate curbs on power. But I think there ought to be some rather more immediate curb than very occasional general elections. In the modern world where things are so closely integrated that is hardly enough, and we ought to have more, I think, in the way of referendums.

WYATT

Don't you think that referendums would be a rather clumsy way of doing this?

RUSSELL

Oh, they'd be clumsy and slow. But I think they might be better than a system in which it's possible at any moment for a government to plunge its country into utter and total disaster without consulting anybody.

7.
What Is Happiness?

7.

WOODROW WYATT

Lord Russell, you seem to be a very happy person. Have you always been so?

LORD RUSSELL

No, certainly not. I've had periods of happiness and periods of unhappiness. Luckily for me the periods of happiness seem to lengthen as I grow older.

WYATT

What was your worst period of unhappiness?

RUSSELL

Well, I was very, very unhappy in adolescence. I think many adolescents are. I had no friends, nobody I could talk to. I thought that I was contemplating suicide all the time and was restraining myself with difficulty from this act and this was not really true. Oh, I certainly imagined that I was very unhappy, but it was partly imaginary, as I discovered from a dream. I dreamed that I was very ill indeed and dying. Oddly enough by my bedside was Professor Jowett, the Master of Balliol and translator of Plato, an extremely learned man who was a friend of my family. He had a very squeaky voice and I in my dream said to him in a very sentimental voice: "Well, at any rate there is one comfort, I shall soon be out of all this," and he said, "Do you mean life?" And I said, "Yes, I mean life," and he said, "When you're a little older you won't talk that sort of nonsense." I woke up and I never talked that sort of nonsense again.

WYATT

But insofar as you have been happy, was this conscious planning, or did it happen by accident?

RUSSELL

Well, there's only been conscious planning as far as my work was concerned, the rest of my life I've left to impulse and accident. But certainly in regard to work I have had a conscious plan which I've carried out pretty well.

WYATT

But leaving happiness to chance and impulse, do you think that works quite well?

RUSSELL

Oh! I think it depends on luck to an enormous degree and also on how your work goes. I had a terrible period of unhappiness at a considerably later time than this adolescence I'm talking of, when I was stumped completely by one problem that I had to solve before I could go on with my work. For two years I struggled with this problem without making any progress whatever and that was very unhappy.

WYATT

What do you think are the ingredients that make for happiness?

RUSSELL

Well, I think four are the most important. Perhaps the first of them is health, the second sufficient means to keep you from want, third happy personal relations, and fourth successful work.

WYATT

Well, what about health? Why do you attach so much importance to that?

RUSSELL

Well, I think if you have certain kinds of ill health it's very difficult indeed to be happy. Certain kinds of ill health affect the mind and cause you to be miserable. Certain other kinds of ill health you can bear stoically, but some you can't.

WYATT

Do you think that being healthy makes you happy, or being happy makes you healthy?

RUSSELL

Well, I think primarily being healthy makes you happy, but the other does work too. I think that a happy man is much less likely to get ill than an unhappy one.

WYATT

You have a happier day, say, the morning after you slept well than on a morning after you slept badly?

RUSSELL

Oh, yes, certainly.

WYATT

Well, can we take the next ingredient, income? How important is that?

RUSSELL

Well, that depends upon the standard you're used to. If you're used to being rather poor, you don't need a very large income. If you're used to being very rich, you feel miserable unless your income is very large, so it's all a question of what you're used to, I think.

WYATT

This can slop over, though, into a kind of obsessional pursuit of money, can't it?

RUSSELL

Oh, very easily, and it often does. You find that the richest men are in terror of dying in the workhouse. That often happens.

WYATT

So too much money doesn't necessarily make for happiness at all.

RUSSELL

No, oh, no. No, I think money is a sort of minimum requirement and you don't want to have to think about it too much. If you have to think about it too much you get worried.

WYATT

You place personal relationships third on the list. Did you mean by that you think it's third in priority?

RUSSELL

Oh, no, no. As far as my experience goes, I should say it's the first requisite, or it's first after health.

WYATT

Will you explain a bit more what you mean by that?

RUSSELL

By personal relations?

WYATT

Yes.

RUSSELL

Oh, well, I should have thought it was fairly obvious what one means. One means friendship, one means love, one means relations with one's children, all those sorts of intimate, close personal relations. If they're unhappy it makes life pretty difficult.

WYATT

Work. Now how high would you place that—the importance of successful work?

RUSSELL

Very high indeed in the case of all energetic people. Some people are more lethargic and don't depend on work so much. But if you are at all energetic you must have an outlet for your energy, and work is the obvious outlet. Of course work won't make you happy if it's unsuccessful. But if it is successful it does fill your day and adds enormously to happiness.

89

WYATT

Does it matter what sort of work?

RUSSELL

No, I don't think it does except that some kinds of work are precarious. I mean, I suppose that if I were a member of the Politburo the work would be a little anxious but—

WYATT

It might provide a stimulus for somebody who liked that sort of thing.

RUSSELL

Yes, if you like that sort of thing it would be all right.

WYATT

But the lowliness or the elevation of the work—is that important?

RUSSELL

Well, no, that depends upon your temperament. Some people can't be happy unless they are engaged in great achievements, others can be quite happy with little achievements. It's a matter of temperament, that. But your work ought to be such as your capacities will enable you to do successfully.

WYATT

What you're saying seems to suggest that one would be fortunate to be lazy, that one can be contented with very much less work.

RUSSELL

Yes, but you wouldn't be as happy, at least as far as my experiences goes. The happiness of a really good successful piece of difficult work is very, very great indeed, and I don't think that the lazy person ever experiences anything equal to it.

WYATT

If you were told that you could have more pleasure if you were less intelligent, how would you react?

RUSSELL

Oh! I wouldn't do it, no. I would indeed be prepared to have less pleasure if I could get a little more intelligence. No, I like intelligence!

WYATT

Do you think that philosophy contributes to happiness?

RUSSELL

Well, it does if you happen to be interested in philosophy and good at it, but not otherwise—but so does bricklaying . . . if you're a good bricklayer. Anything you're good at contributes to happiness.

WYATT

What are the factors that militate against happiness?

RUSSELL

Well, there are quite a number, apart from the opposites of the things we're talking about. Now one of the things that militates against happiness is worry, and that's one respect in which I've become much happier as I've grown older. I worry much less and I found a very useful plan in regard to worry, which is to think, "Now what is the very worst thing that could happen?" . . . And then think, "Well, after all it wouldn't be so very bad a hundred years hence; it probably wouldn't matter." After you've really made yourself think that, you won't worry so much. Worry comes from not facing unpleasant possibilities.

WYATT

Are you able to shut out worry at will?

RUSSELL

Not completely, no, but to a very great extent.

WYATT

Where would you place envy?

RUSSELL

Oh. Envy, yes. It's a terrible source of unhappiness to a great many people. I remember the painter Haydon, who wasn't a very good painter but wished he was. He kept a diary and in it he records, "Spent a miserable morning comparing myself with Raphael."

WYATT

Would you elaborate this question of envy a bit more?

RUSSELL

I think a great many people who have quite a lot that might make them happy worry because somebody else seems to have a bit more. They think that somebody else has a better car or a better garden, or how nice it would be to live in a happier climate, or how much more recognition so-and-so's work gets—things like that. Instead of enjoying what is there for them to enjoy, the pleasure of it is taken away by the thought that perhaps somebody else has more, which ought not to matter.

WYATT

Yes, but mightn't envy be a good thing in the sense that if you envy somebody else's work because you think it may be better than yours, it might be a stimulant to you to do your own work better?

RUSSELL

Yes, it might, but it also adds a stimulus to do worse work, I think, and above all to try to interfere with the other person's work. There are two ways of getting ahead of the other man, one is to get ahead yourself, and the other is to keep him back.

WYATT

Boredom . . . How important do you think boredom is?

RUSSELL

I think it's enormously important, and I think it's—I won't say it's distinctly human, because I've looked at apes in the zoo and they seemed to me to be experiencing boredom—but I don't think other animals are bored. I think it's a mark of higher intelligence, but I think the importance of it is quite enormous. You can see it from the way that savages, when they first come in contact with civilized people, want above all things alcohol. They want it far more than they want the Bible or the Gospel, or even blue beads, and they want it because for a moment it takes away boredom.

WYATT

But how is one to overcome boredom in people, say, girls who are quite well educated? They marry and then have nothing else to do but look after the house.

RUSSELL

Well, it's a bad social system. I don't think that you can always alter it by individual action, but that example you give is nowadays very important. It shows that we haven't got a proper social system because everybody ought to be able to exercise whatever useful skill he or she possesses. Modern highly educated women after they marry are not so very well able to, but that's an effect of our social system.

WYATT

How far does it help one to be happy to understand one's own motives for doing things, and so avoid self-deception?

RUSSELL

Oh, I think it helps a great deal. All sorts of people take up either the hatred of some person or the hatred of some group of persons, or something, under the impression that it's a noble idealism that is prompting them. When in fact it may very likely not be. If they could realize that, I think they would be happier.

WYATT

Do you think a lot of people are made unhappy by deceiving themselves?

RUSSELL

Oh, yes, I think a very great many.

WYATT

Do you think it's possible to be happy in adversity—in prison, say. You were in there yourself.

RUSSELL

Oh, well, I had a very pleasant time in jail, but then I was in the first division where they didn't inflict the ordinary hardships of prison life at all. But ordinarily it's very, very difficult for a man accustomed to mental work. It's much easier if you're accustomed to manual work, because you're not deprived so much of your mental life.

WYATT

Do you think it's easier to be happier, say, in prison in the situation that you were in—when you thought you were in for a good cause—than if you're in because you deserve it.

RUSSELL

Oh, certainly it is. I mean, if they'd given me the same sentence for stealing spoons, I should have been quite unhappy because I should have felt . . . well . . . well, I've been deservedly disgraced. But as it was I didn't feel disgraced.

WYATT

Simply because it was a matter of principle?

RUSSELL

Yes.

WYATT

Do you think that it helps people to be happy to have some cause to live for and with?

RUSSELL

Yes, provided they can succeed more or less. I think if it's a cause in which there is no success they don't get happy. But if they can get a measure of success from time to time, then I think it does help. And I think I should go on from that to another thing, which is that side interests, especially as one gets older, are a very important element in happiness. The more your interests are impersonal and extend beyond your own life, the less you will mind the prospect that your own life may be going to come to an end before very long. I think that's a very important element of happiness in old age.

WYATT

What do you think of all these formulae that people are constantly issuing about how to live a long life and be happy?

RUSSELL

Well, as to how to live a longer life, that's a medical question and not one on which I should like to express an opinion. I get a great deal of literature from the advocates of these systems. They tell me that if only I took their drugs my hair would turn black again. I'm not sure that I should like that because I find that the whiter my hair becomes the more ready people are to believe what I say.

8.

Nationalism

8.

WOODROW WYATT

Do you think that nationalism is a good or a bad thing, Lord Russell?

LORD RUSSELL

One would have to distinguish between cultural and political aspects of nationalism. From the cultural point of view one of the rather sad things about the modern world is its extraordinary uniformity. If you go to an expensive hotel, there's nothing whatever to show you which continent it's in or which part of the world or anything; they are all exactly alike over the whole world, and that gets a little dull and makes rich travelling really hardly worth doing. If you want to see foreign countries you have to travel poor, and in that respect I think there's a great deal to be said for nationalism. For keeping diversity—in literature, in art, in language, and all kinds of cultural things. But when it comes to politics, I think nationalism is unmitigatedly evil. I don't think there is a single thing to be said in its favour.

WYATT

Well, what would you say are the purposes—the main purposes—of the organization of a national state?

RUSSELL

Well, the main purposes are what a state itself calls "defense"—and what all other states call "aggression." It's the same phenomenon only it has different names from two sides. In fact the state is primarily an organization for killing foreigners, that's its main purpose. There are, of course, other things they do. They do a certain amount of educating, but in the course of educating you try very hard to make the young think it is a grand thing to kill foreigners. I mean, take, for instance, that verse in the national anthem which they don't sing as often as they did when I was young, where it says, "Confound their navish tricks, frustrate their politics and make them fall." We all used to sing that with great gusto about every foreigner.

WYATT

Like "Rule, Britannia!"?

RUSSELL

Well "Britannia" also. Now since Britannia ceased to rule the waves, we can't very well say, "Rule, the United States, the United States rule the waves" because it won't scan. And so we've dropped the whole thing.

WYATT

That's the sort of thing you mean by nationalism being harmful?

RUSSELL

What I mean by it being harmful is that it's a part of its teaching to inculcate the view that your own country is glorious and has always been right in everything, whereas other countries—well, as Mr. Podsnap says in Dickens, "Foreign nations, I am sorry to say, do as they do." I don't thing that it's right to view foreign nations in that way. One sees curious examples of it. I wrote a book in which I was talking about nationalism, and I said, "There is, of course, one nation which has all the supreme virtues that every nation arrogates to itself. That one is the one to which my reader belongs." And I got a letter from a Pole saying, "I'm so glad you recognize the superiority of Poland."

WYATT

Yes, I see. Well, what other sort of occasion do you think this arises in—I mean, can you give any more illustrations of it?

RUSSELL

Yes. There was a very charming young lady at a meeting of the United Nations who was much given to riding a bicycle. She came from Ecuador, and her bicycle ran away with her down a very steep hill, and she might easily have been killed. And my friend, Gilbert Murray, asked her, "Were you not frightened when your bicycle ran away with you?" And she said, "Oh, no. I said to myself, remember that you are an Ecuadorian!"

WYATT

But this of course could apply to anybody.

RUSSELL

Yes. I used to tell this story sometimes and everybody laughed. And I would say, "Yes, but you know if I'd mention a certain other country, nobody would have laughed."

WYATT

Yes. Why do people want to be divided up into national states?

RUSSELL

Well, it is part of our emotional apparatus that we are liable to both love and hate, and we like to exercise them. We love our compatriots and we hate foreigners. Of course we love our compatriots only when we're thinking of foreigners. When we've forgotten foreigners we don't love them so much.

WYATT

But then what would you do about this? You're saying that a certain amount of nationalism is agreeable and right. How are you going to make sure that it doesn't go too far?

RUSSELL

Well, I don't think you can; you can never make sure of these things. But what you can say and what the world will have to say if man is to survive is that armies and navies and air forces should not be national but international. Then it won't much matter if you think ill of some other country provided you're not in a position to kill them off.

WYATT

I'm getting at something else. Sometimes if you feel you're doing a thing for your country, say, like climbing Mount Everest or developing some machine to fly to outer space, you may be inspired to do it more vigorously and effectively than if you think you're doing it on a kind of vague global basis.

RUSSELL

Well, it's quite true people want a rather narrower stimulus—but I think there are plenty of ways of keeping that. I mean, take a thing like the Everest expedition, it's not only a country that does it, but almost always some institute or some collection of very rich men or something of that sort, and you can do it for their glory just as well as for the glory of your country.

WYATT

But if you're going to have some kind of rivalry and stimulus in a competitive way surely the nation is really a convenient way to do it?

RUSSELL

Yes. I don't mind at all having competition and emulation provided it doesn't involve killing. I think that municipal rivalry is all right. If one city builds a very fine town hall, another thinks, "We must have a fine town hall." Well, all that's sort of to the good. Manchester and Liverpool, I understand, don't love each other, but they haven't got private armies to go to war with each other.

WYATT

Well, now how are you going to run an orderly society, particularly in times of danger, crisis, and tension, if you don't believe in the proposition, "My country right or wrong"?

RUSSELL

Well, if one's talking now of what ought to be the case, there ought, as I said before, to be only one armed force, which should be international and not national. In that case these situations of danger that you're talking of wouldn't arise, because there would be no opportunity for national aggression, and therefore no need for national defense.

WYATT

But they do arise at the moment?

RUSSELL

They do arise at the moment, and so you've got to get into people's heads that while it's quite proper to resist aggression it is not proper to commit aggression. If nobody committed aggression the occasion for resisting aggression would not arise. But I do think resisting aggression is quite a proper thing to do.

WYATT

Take the Middle East since the end of the last war. Now there Arab nationalism has thrown up a lot of new states and has given a great deal of self-confidence and a sense of well-being to a large number of Arabs. Now is that good or bad?

RUSSELL

Well, it's very difficult as yet to say. I think insofar as it involves raising the self-respect of Arabs and making Arabs think they're capable of great achievements—in all that it's good. But insofar as it involves hatred of people who are not Arabs, for example, the people of Israel, it can't be considered good.

WYATT

What I don't understand is how one is somehow to put within bounds nationalist feelings, having once aroused them to worthy causes. How do you stop them slopping over into bad ones?

RUSSELL

Simply through unifying the Governments. Now take the case of England and Scotland. England and Scotland went to war with each other for centuries—for centuries—and it was universally held on each side of the Border that it was proper to hate the people on the other side of the Border. And then from a pure dynastic accident the governments were unified, and this hatred ceased.

WYATT

You mean they happened to have the same king?

RUSSELL

Yes.

WYATT

By mistake?

RUSSELL

Yes.

WYATT

How far would you say racial prejudice is connected with nationalism?

RUSSELL

Well, it comes in of course. I mean it comes in if there is a racial difference between two neighbouring nations. Racial prejudice comes in and intensifies the nationalism of each. It is not the same thing—racial prejudice is not the same thing as nationalism, but it very easily gets allied with it.

WYATT

Would you say that racial prejudice has very much increased over the last fifty years?

RUSSELL

Yes, I suppose it has, but I'm not quite sure. I . . . I don't know—I mean, take, for instance, Rudyard Kipling, who did a great deal to stimulate British imperialism. He talked about the "lesser breeds without the law," and all his writings were concerned with suggesting that anybody who wasn't white—or one might almost say anybody who wasn't British—was somewhat inferior, so that I don't think it's so recent as all that.

WYATT

We all know that Americans and Europeans suffer from racial prejudice. Do you think that Asians and Africans suffer from racial prejudice any less?

RUSSELL

Not a bit less. And in fact because it's rather new with them they probably suffer more at the present moment. I should think that both African and Asian nationalism are, at the moment, more fierce than any that exist among Europeans, because they've just awakened to it. I think it is a very, very great danger. I think nationalism is, apart from the tension and the danger of an East-West war, I think nationalism is the greatest danger that man is faced with at the present time.

WYATT

Do you think people sometimes assume that when other nations are being treated badly those nations are really rather splendid people? To a greater extent than they actually are?

RUSSELL

Oh, certainly they do. It's a fixed pattern that when some nation or class or whatnot is unjustly oppressed, people with decent humanitarian feelings begin to think they must be perfectly virtuous and altogether delightful people. And then, of course, in the end they get free and as soon as they get free they devote themselves, as far as their power goes, to practising all the vices that previously were practised by their oppressors.

WYATT

Is this an inevitable pattern?

RUSSELL

No, no. It's not inevitable, and it doesn't always happen. I . . . I think one must take India as a case of how it doesn't always happen. I think India, since it became free, has been singularly without that sort of vice which so often happens to liberated peoples.

WYATT

Why do you think nationalism seems to be so much more virulent today than it ever has been before?

RUSSELL

Oh, it's due to education. Education has done an awful lot of harm. I sometimes think it would've been better if people were still unable to read and write. Because the great majority, when they learn to read and write, become open to propaganda, and in each country the propaganda is controlled by the state and is what the state likes. And what the state likes is to have you quite ready to commit murder when you're told to.

WYATT

Now you were saying a moment ago that you thought nationalism was about the worst thing there was in the world. Do you mean that you think it's even a greater danger than communism?

RUSSELL

Well, I don't think it is a greater danger than the East-West tension is; that, I think is the greatest danger in the world. But I think that if the East-West tension was removed, it would be. Nationalism would threaten mankind more than the peaceful extension of communism would do.

WYATT

Is there any solution to this problem of nationalism other than having, say, an imminent invasion from Mars?

RUSSELL

Well, that of course would stop it at once. We should then have planetary nationalism for our planet against all other planets. We should teach in schools how much more noble our planet has always been than these wretched Martians, of whom we shouldn't know anything and therefore we could imagine any number of vices, so that would be a very simple solution. But I'm afraid we may not be able to do it that way. I think we've got to hope that people will get positive aims—aims of promoting the welfare of their own and other countries, rather than these negative aims of strife.

9.
Great Britain

9.

WOODROW WYATT

Lord Russell, do you think we've got about the right sort of mixture between capitalism and socialism in Great Britain?

LORD RUSSELL

Yes, I do. I think we've got the right mixture for the present time, but I don't say it'll be the right mixture forever because I think circumstances change. My view has been for a long time now that when any particular kind of economic activity has reached the stage of monopoly, it is better run by the state than by private enterprise, and that is partly what we've got now in England.

WYATT

Do you think this is tolerably fair all round?

RUSSELL

Yes, I think it's as fair as you can make it. It isn't perfectly fair, but nothing is.

WYATT

What would you say are the main virtues of British society?

RUSSELL

Well, I should put first and foremost a certain kind of diffused kindliness. I don't say in dealings with people who are not British—that's a different matter; but internally, I think, the British are more kindly than most people that I've come across.

WYATT

Could you explain that a bit?

RUSSELL

Yes, I should like to. I . . . I don't think they have the same inflexible dogmas that are very common in other countries. And I think partly owing to the fact that we haven't had a foreign invasion since 1066, we haven't got so much reason for savagery in our history as most countries have.

WYATT

Do you think that the British are better than most other people in devising a good system of justice?

RUSSELL

Well, I don't know exactly what one means by justice. Do you mean the law, or do you mean economic justice?

WYATT

Well, both really.

RUSSELL

I think complete economic justice would be really difficult to get and is perhaps hardly desirable. I think we have come as near it as one can hope to do, and certainly very much nearer than they have come to it in Communist countries where the differences between rich and poor are much greater than they are here.

WYATT

What about legal justice and fair dealing?

RUSSELL

Well, I don't suppose we're perfect—no country is—but I think we're as good as anybody is.

WYATT

How about our ability to compromise that we're so proud of?

RUSSELL

I think it is perhaps our greatest virtue. We didn't always have it. We didn't have it in the seventeenth century and we suffered great troubles in consequence. But in 1688 we decided that we didn't want any more of these troubles; we adopted the plan of always compromising, which has worked extremely well. For example, when the French Revolution came French aristocrats were asked, "Would you rather surrender your privileges or have your heads cut off?" and they said, "Naturally, have our heads cut off," and they did. Whereas in England in 1832, the Reform Bill before Parliament involved the surrender of the privileges of the aristocracy. My grandfather himself, very much an aristocrat, brought in the bill and got it through.

WYATT

That was Lord John Russell?

RUSSELL

Yes. And I think I may attribute to him the fact that my head is still on my shoulders.

WYATT

How does this differ from the continental approach?

RUSSELL

The continental approach is much more rigid. You are for this or for that and not for getting a suitable adjustment of the two. I can give you an illustration of that from philosophy. At one time I was living at Princeton in America and Einstein lived there, and I used to go once a week to his house and meet him and see other very eminent German intellectuals. They were all Jews, they were all exiles from Germany, bitterly hostile to the Nazi regime and as liberal as you could wish. We used to debate fundamental questions of philosophy and we had every wish to agree—there was nothing combative in any of us. But always when we got down to fundamentals there was a gulf that we couldn't cross. They stood for a certain kind of mystical idealism, and I stood for hardheaded empiricism, and we couldn't get across it.

WYATT

Would you say that you yourself were in the British tradition?

RUSSELL

Oh, very much so. You see, the British tradition comes primarily from Locke; Locke partly imbued the three great British philosophers. When I was young the British universities had been invaded by German idealism, but when the Germans invaded Belgium it was decided that the German philosophy must be bad. And so I came into my own, because I was against German philosophy anyhow.

WYATT

Do you feel yourself to be British?

RUSSELL

Indeed yes, and quite in the tradition.

WYATT

Do you think that tradition has played a large part in Britain's ability to keep herself afloat in a reasonable and stable way?

RUSSELL

Yes, I do. I . . . I think we like tradition unless it does some very obvious harm. Now take, for instance, the question of the naming of streets. In every continental country that I know of they change the streets every now and again because their politics have changed, and the great men they used to admire they no longer admire. If we were like the continentals we should knock down the Duke of York's column, because we don't admire the Duke of York.

WYATT

What other sort of things have you got in mind in speaking of tradition?

RUSSELL

Well, all sorts of ways of going on. Formulae that people use in the law courts or they use in writs summoning people to Parliament—all kinds of little bits of tradition which most English people very much like and don't want to see swept away.

What about that peculiar institution of which you're a member, the House of Lords?

RUSSELL

Well, the House of Lords, of course, is peculiar. I don't know that I could really undertake to defend it because it is so very queer, but I do rather enjoy it all the same.

WYATT

What about monarchy, do you think that plays a large part?

RUSSELL

Yes, the monarchy I'm all for. Very much for. If you don't have a monarchy you have to have a president and it's an awful job electing one. Then anyway people don't always like him; half the nation doesn't like him, or nearly half. But as a monarch we can all like him and it is much more preferable. I very much like it better.

WYATT

Have you always been respectful to the monarchy?

RUSSELL

Oh, yes, I started at a very early age. When I was two years old Queen Victoria came to see my people, and they recorded with surprise how very respectfully I behaved to her.

WYATT

What about history? Do you think the sense of history in Britain partly stems from the monarchy?

RUSSELL

Well, I don't know how much it does because all that sense of history was already in the people who were against the monarchy. I read at one time a lot of Roundhead literature at the time of the British Civil War, and they thought then of the aristocracy as Norman and foreign. They were very much imbued with history although they were revolutionaries.

WYATT

Is it important for a nation, do you think, to have a sense of history?

RUSSELL

Yes, I think it's enormously important; it gives stability, and it gives depth to your thought and to your feeling.

WYATT

Do you think we've got that?

RUSSELL

We have it in England very much indeed, yes; and of course it's encouraged by the existence of old buildings, the existence of Roman remains, and all sorts of things. There's a great deal that encourages a sense of history in this country, and I'm very glad there is.

WYATT

Would you agree that Britain is one of the most snobbish countries in the world?

RUSSELL

Oh, certainly. Well, not quite, perhaps, the most snobbish that I've ever struck. I . . . I've come across a certain amount of snobbery in the Western Hemisphere that seemed to me, if anything, to surpass what I know at home. But certainly there is a very great deal of snobbery in this country. A very great deal.

WYATT

Do you think it does harm?

RUSSELL

Yes, it does some harm. It does some harm and some good. I mean, insofar as the people whom the snob admires are better than he is, it does good; insofar as they are only conventionally better, it does harm.

WYATT

Can you give me an illustration of what you mean by snobbery?

RUSSELL

I remember an old fellow of King's in my day; his name was Oscar Browning, and he certainly was a snob. The Empress Frederick came to Cambridge one day and I regret to say there was another fellow at King's whom she liked better, and Oscar Browning trotted round the university all day. I met him late in the evening quite exhausted and he said, "I've been Empress hunting all day."

WYATT

I remember you telling me one about a man called Cave.

RUSSELL

Oh, yes, that was an example of working with snobbery. My people lived in Richmond Park and I was brought up there. There was a man called Cave, who was a prominent citizen of Richmond, and some of the inhabitants of Richmond thought that he ought to be given a knighthood. And they went round getting up a petition that he should be given a knighthood, and they came to my grandmother, the Prime Minister's widow, and she said: "Oh, no, this is a matter for the sovereign." She couldn't possibly consider that she ought to try to influence the sovereign in such a matter, and so she refused to sign the petition. Well, later on Cave's son became Home Secretary and sent me to jail. However, I profited a bit from all this snobbery because my brother used to demand this and that privilege for me, and he said, "Of course, young Cave will have to do it because he was my fag at Winchester."

WYATT

And did he?

RUSSELL

He did. Oh, yes.

WYATT

Do you think America will ever become like Britain?

RUSSELL

No, I don't for several reasons. The most important reason is that the proportion of Americans of British descent is continually diminishing. But apart from that there are other reasons. One is that America hasn't got the same roots in the past that any European country has. Another is that the British who went to America originally were the British who couldn't stand the British quality of loving compromise. They were extremists who couldn't get on with her and they established a somewhat different sort of mentality from ours. Another is that the early settlers were constantly engaged in fighting the Indians and that caused a certain strain.

WYATT

Is our democratic approach a matter of history, or temperament, or climate, or what?

RUSSELL

I think it's a matter of history most of all, and I think perhaps the most important element in it is the fact that we haven't had a foreign invasion since 1066. Practically every country on the Continent has had foreign invaders, and foreign invaders have a very, very bad effect on the mentality of the people who suffer them.

WYATT

Do you think that the aristocrats of 1832 understood what it was that your grandfather was trying to do for them with his Reform Act?

RUSSELL

Well, half of them did and half of them didn't, but the half that did not was patiently waiting to get the thing through. I think the half that did understand, understood extremely well.

WYATT

Do you think that's why the upper classes of Britain have gone on making compromises so that they won't lose their privileges?

RUSSELL

I think so, yes. To avoid having revolutions, and having their heads cut off, and all that sort of thing. It occurred to them that's what will happen if they're not sensible.

WYATT

Do you think they're still doing that?

RUSSELL

Oh, yes, certainly.

WYATT

Do you think it matters about Great Britain not being one of the really great powers any more?

RUSSELL

Well, of course my natural feeling is to regret it. I mean, I have the ordinary patriotic feelings and I'm sorry in that way. But when I try to think impersonally I don't know that it really matters very much.

WYATT

Why do you think it doesn't matter?

RUSSELL

Well, I think that the peculiar virtues of the British were more displayed at home than they were abroad, and I don't know that we were so very much better than other people would be in our dealings either with foreign nations or with subject populations. That's one reason. Another reason is that, well, I suppose there's got to be some nations more powerful than others.

123

WYATT

Do you think that the ones that have become more power-ful than us will make a better job of it?

RUSSELL

No, I don't think they'll make a better job. I hope that at any rate America may make as good a job, but I don't expect to see them make a better job.

WYATT

How do you see the future of Great Britain?

RUSSELL

I see the future of Great Britain on the analogy of what happened in Holland. Holland was a great power in the seventeenth century and then it ceased to be a great power; but it ceased without disaster. It ceased without any parti-cular catastrophe and settled down quite well to be a very civilized and a very respectable minor power, and I think that's what we must hope to do.

WYATT

Could you describe the sort of society that might occur in Britain under this dispensation?

RUSSELL

Well, I don't know. I suppose it will go on more or less like what it is at present, with elements of tradition ming-ling rather oddly with socialistic elements. I think that they'll both go on surviving.

WYATT

Do you think Britain will continue to exert a strong moral influence in the world?

RUSSELL

Well, I should like to think so. But that depends upon our politicians, and I don't know what sort of politicians we're going to get.

10.
The Role of the
Individual

IO.

WOODROW WYATT

What do you mean by the role of the individual?

LORD RUSSELL

I'm thinking primarily of activities which an individual can carry out otherwise than as a member of an organization. I think there are a great many very important and very useful, desirable activities which have hitherto been carried out by individuals without the help of an organization, and which are coming more and more to depend upon organizations. The great men of science of the past didn't depend upon very expensive apparatus—great men like Copernicus, Galileo, Newton, Darwin. They did their work as individuals, and they were able to. But take a modern astronomer. I met a very eminent astronomer of the present day when I was in California, and his work, which is very useful and lovely work, depends entirely upon certain very, very powerful telescopes, which have been contributed to a certain observatory by a certain very rich man. And he explained to me during dinner, that of course he was only able to do his work because he was on good terms with certain very, very rich men.

WYATT

What is your solution?

RUSSELL

Well, I don't think there is any solution to that particular problem except a general interested desire for the furthering of knowledge. And I think that is a large hope, but I don't see what else you can do.

WYATT

How is anyone to establish a claim or a right to use this tremendously expensive equipment?

RUSSELL

Well, you can only use it through the vote of colleagues. Fortunately in science it is fairly easy to assess a man's ability. In art it's a quite different thing. A poet or a painter or an architect if he pleases his contemporaries is not likely to be an important innovator; yet the important innovators displease their contemporaries so that in art it's very difficult.

WYATT

But may one go a little further into cultural and scientific freedom and what precisely it means in its importance to the community?

RUSSELL

Well, I came to the conclusion a little while ago that broadly speaking the important impulses that promote behaviour can be divided into creative and possessive. I call an impulse creative when its aim is to produce something which wouldn't otherwise be there and is not taken away from anybody else. I call it possessive when it consists in acquiring for yourself something which is already there, such as a loaf of bread. Now of course both have their function and man has to be sufficiently possessive to keep himself alive, but the really important impulses, when you're talking about the sphere of liberty, are the creative ones. If you write a poem you don't prevent another man from writing a poem. If you paint a picture you don't prevent another from painting a picture. Those things are creative and are not done at the expense of somebody else, and I think those things ought to have absolute liberty.

WYATT

Do you believe that cultural and scientific freedom is declining?

RUSSELL

Yes, it is almost inevitably declining; not, I think, perhaps so much in artistic spheres, but certainly in scientific spheres,—for the reason I spoke of before. The apparatus in science is now so expensive that a man can't be a Galileo with his own telescope. You can't make a modern telescope yourself.

WYATT

Yes, but surely there's a great advantage today in that many people who made scientific discoveries in the past were in danger of having their heads chopped off; whereas today you can carry on.

RUSSELL

I don't think that's quite true. We don't as a rule chop off their heads, but if they get into bad odour politically, as they very well may, they don't have access to the necessary laboratories.

WYATT

But has scientific freedom and cultural freedom ever really existed?

RUSSELL

No, I don't think so. No, I don't think it ever has. In fact the people who make any important advance in any direction whatever almost invariably rouse immense public opposition.

WYATT

Can you give us some examples of that?

RUSSELL

Copernicus. You take Galileo. They both got into hot water for their discoveries. And Darwin, of course, was thought of as unspeakably wicked in his own day. Almost anybody who makes an important advance is so thought.

WYATT

Isn't it quite a good thing that when people do offer propositions which may or may not be important advances, they should meet a lot of opposition? Then they can be tested and we don't have a lot of phoney theories foisted on us.

RUSSELL

Well, I don't think it prevents phoney theories, because governments in every part of the world that I have ever heard of prefer phoney theories and they promote them. The theories that are valid will have to meet with violent opposition. Now, I think there is this much to be said for your point. If the opposition is not very severe it is a stimulus, but if it's very severe it isn't. If your head is cut off it immensely diminishes your thinking power.

WYATT

Why is it, do you think, so many discoveries have shocked people?

RUSSELL

Because they make people feel unsafe. Every human being, like every animal, wants to live in what is felt to be a safe environment—an environment where you won't be exposed to unexpected perils. Now when a man tells you that something you've always believed was in fact not true, it gives you a frightful shock and you think, "Oh! I don't know where I am. When I think I'm planting my foot upon the ground, perhaps I'm not. And you get into a terror.

WYATT

Well, this really affects discoveries in the realm of thought rather than in practical science. I mean, nobody minds if somebody invents a machine that will go to the moon.

RUSSELL

Well, no. But they do mind—at least some people mind, though not as many as I should have expected—a machine that would destroy the human race, which is also part of science.

WYATT

Yes, but that is rather a different thing, isn't it? I mean, many new discoveries, like television, say, haven't really shocked people.

RUSSELL

Well, that's a new invention, but the discoveries upon which new inventions are based very often have effects in the realm of thought as opposed to the realm of technics, and those are generally rather shocking to most people.

WYATT

You attach enormous importance to this question of the role of the individual. Why have you attached so much importance to it?

RUSSELL

Because all the important human advances that we know of since historical times began have been due to individuals of whom the majority faced virulent public opposition.

WYATT

Do you think that fear of public opinion has stopped many people from doing good and sensible things?

RUSSELL

Yes, it has a very profound effect, especially in times of excitement when there's a great deal of mass hysteria about. A great many people are terrified of going against mass hysteria with the result that bad things triumph where they shouldn't.

WYATT

Do you think that applies to scientists and artists?

RUSSELL

Yes, I think so. I think scientists have the prerogative that they are sometimes able to prove that they're right; but artists can't prove that they are right. An artist can only hope that other people will think so; so I think the artist is in a greater difficulty than the scientist. But the scientist in the modern world undoubtedly is in difficulty, because he may make discoveries that are inconvenient to the government and in that case he'll get into trouble.

WYATT

Oh, do you think he couldn't get away with it in the Western world?

RUSSELL

He might or might not. It would depend partly upon his eminence, partly upon the degree of proof that he had, and partly upon the degree of inconvenience that it would cause to the administration.

WYATT

Well, what about people who are in a sense thinkers and not strictly either artists or scientists devising practical things?

RUSSELL

Well, of course that depends. A great many thinkers do take care not to express in any public way opinions which will bring them obloquy.

WYATT

What about people outside those categories?

RUSSELL

Take a very notable case which happened in America after the First World War. There were two men, Sacco and

135

Vanzetti, who were accused of murder. The evidence was quite inadequate, and after they'd been condemned a small body of people was appointed to look into the evidence. Among them was the President of Harvard and he and the others judged that the men were guilty and they were executed. I think everybody who looked into the evidence at all impartially thought that it was not such as should have lead to a condemnation.

WYATT

Even the President of Harvard, you mean, knew that they were not guilty?

RUSSELL

I think he must have known. I cannot say, because I cannot read his soul. But I think he must have known.

WYATT

And it was only public opinion?

RUSSELL

Yes.

WYATT

Now we are getting very close to this whole topic of the amount of liberty that the individual ought to sacrifice in order to have an orderly society. What do you say about that?

RUSSELL

Well, I do think that the preservation of social order is essential. You must have, if you can, a world in which people don't steal, in which they don't kill each other, and so forth, and to some degree you secure that internally by means of the police. I think those sorts of limitations on liberty are quite necessary, especially in a very crowded community. Take, for example, the rule of the road. When I was young there were no motorcars about; you could drive about as you liked; you didn't have to bother. Now there is a very elaborate code which you have to obey and if you do not, it will cause a great deal of trouble both to yourself and other people. That is because there is more crowding in the world in general, and I think certain national liberties which in the past were immensely valued have become harmful, just as it would be if you had no rule of the road.

WYATT

Do you think any new limitations on liberty are needed?

RUSSELL

Yes, certainly. Limitations on national liberty are needed and there are some things that are absurd. The arguments that socialists used in favour of nationalizing natural resources have now become arguments in favour of internationalizing natural resources. The most obvious example is oil. It's a little absurd that a very small territory which happens to have a great deal of oil on its territory should be the sole possessor of that oil.

WYATT

Do you think liberties need expanding?

RUSSELL

Well, liberties need enlarging in a mental sphere and, if anything, diminishing in what I call the possessive sphere.

II.

Fanaticism and Tolerance

II.

WOODROW WYATT

What is your definition of fanaticism, Lord Russell?

LORD RUSSELL

I should be inclined to say that a man is a fanatic if he thinks some one matter so overwhelmingly important that it outweighs anything else at all. To take an example, I suppose all decent people dislike cruelty to dogs, but if you thought that cruelty to dogs was so atrocious that no other cruelty should be objected to in comparison, then you would be a fanatic.

WYATT

Do you think this has happened a great deal in human history—that large groups of people have been seized with fanaticism?

RUSSELL

Yes, it's happened at most periods in most parts of the world. It's one of the diseases of the mind to which communities are subject.

WYATT

Which would you say are some of the worst occasions?

RUSSELL

Well, I think there have been various occasions one could mention. Take anti-Semitism. That is one of the most dreadful because that is the worst manifestation that is recent, and so dreadful one can hardly bear to think of it. Well, though I know it is not the right thing to say—it is not considered the right thing to say—anti-Semitism came in with Christianity; before that there was very, very much less. The moment the Roman government became Christian it began to be anti-Semitic.

WYATT

Why was that?

RUSSELL

Because they said that the Jews killed Christ and so it became a justification for hating the Jews. I have no doubt there really were economic motives, but that was the justification.

WYATT

Why do you think people do get seized in large numbers with fanaticism?

RUSSELL

Well, it's partly that it gives you a cosy feeling of co-operation. A fanatical group all together have a comfortable feeling that they're all friends with one another. They are all very much excited about the same thing. You can see it in any political party. There's always a fringe of fanatics in any political party, and they feel very cosy with one another and when that is spread about and is combined with a propensity to hate some other group you get fanaticism well developed.

But might fanaticism at times provide a kind of mainspring for good actions?

It provides a mainspring for actions all right, but I can't think of any instance in history where it's provided the mainspring for good actions. Always I think it has been for bad ones because it is partial, because it almost inevitably involves some kind of hatred. You hate the people who don't share your fanaticism. It's almost inevitable.

Then if it gets taken over by economic considerations, say, like the Crusades, then fanaticism disappears and perhaps does no harm?

Well, I don't know. I . . . I can't think of any good that the Crusades did. The Crusades had, of course, two different streams in them: a fanatical stream and an economic stream. The economic stream was very strong indeed, but it wouldn't have worked without the fanaticism. The fanaticism provided the troops, and the economic motive the generals, roughly speaking.

But what part would you say that witchcraft has played in fanaticism?

RUSSELL

Oh, witchcraft played a terrible, terrible part, especially from . . . oh . . . from about 1450 to a little beyond 1600. Quite a terrible part. There was a work called *The Hammer of Female Malefactors,* written by an eminent ecclesiastic, and inspired the most mad profusion of witch hunts, which the people themselves believed. I think it's very likely that Joan of Arc believed she was a witch. Certainly a great many people condemned as witches did believe they were witches, and there was an enormous spread of cruelty. Now Sir Thomas Browne, you would say when you read his works, seems like a very humane and cultivated person; but he actually took part in trials of witches on the side of the prosecution, and he said that to deny witchcraft is a form of atheism, because after all the Bible says, Thou shalt not suffer a witch to live. Therefore, if you don't think it's right to burn them if you think they're witches, you must be disbelieving in the Bible and therefore be an atheist.

WYATT

Why is it that many people who are quite sane, on the surface at any rate, are so fanatical?

RUSSELL

Well, sanity is a relative term. Very, very few people are sane all through. Almost everybody has corners where they're mad. I remember once I was motoring in California on a very, very wet day and we picked up a pedestrian who was getting wet through, and he railed against all kinds of race prejudice. He said it was a most dreadful thing, and

I entirely agreed with him. Then somebody mentioned the Philippines, and he said all Filipinos are vile. Well, you see he had that little corner of insanity.

WYATT

Why do you attach so much importance to the subject of fanaticism?

RUSSELL

Because a very great part of the evils that the world is suffering are due to fanaticism.

WYATT

But then the Roman Catholic Church, for example, presumably thought that it was more important that you should believe certain dogmas than remain alive if you didn't. Is there no difference between that and what we think today?

RUSSELL

The difference is one of scope. The Roman Catholic Church was not world-wide. There were a great many people that it couldn't catch, but the H-bomb could catch everybody.

WYATT

Well, can you elaborate on that?

RUSSELL

Yes, certainly. It deserves to be elaborated. I think that the East-West tension which is threatening us all in the most terrible fashion is mainly due to fanatical belief in Communism or anti-Communism, as the case may be. Both sides believe their own creed too strongly. They believe it in the way that I defined as fanatical; that is to say, the prevention of what they regard as wicked on the other side is more important even than the continued existence of the human race—and that is fanatical. It is that fanaticism which is threatening us all, a fanaticism which exists on both sides.

WYATT

What is your definition of toleration?

RUSSELL

Well, it varies according to the direction of your thinking. Toleration of opinion, if it's really full-blown, consists in not punishing any kind of opinion as long as it doesn't issue in some kind of criminal action.

WYATT

Can you give some illustrations of periods in history which have been tolerant?

RUSSELL

Yes. It really does begin with the end of the Thirty Years' War. It didn't begin in England until a little later, because we were in the middle of our Civil War at the time, but it began very soon after that. The first really tolerant state was Holland. All the leading intellects of the seventeenth century at some period of their lives had to take refuge in Holland, and if there hadn't been Holland they'd have been wiped out. The English were no better than other people at that time. There was a parliamentary investigation which decided that Hobbes was very, very wicked and it was decreed that no work by Hobbes was to be published in England. And it wasn't for a long, long time.

Would you say that ancient Athens was a tolerant state?

It was more or less tolerant. It was more tolerant than modern states were until the eighteenth century. But it was not of course completely tolerant. Everybody knows about Socrates being put to death, and apart from him there were other people. Anaxagoras had to fly. Aristotle had to fly after the death of Alexander. They were not thoroughly tolerant by any means.

Then how is one to know when one's got to a tolerant period? How does one recognize this?

Well, you recognize it by the liberal freedoms. Free press, free thought, free propaganda. Freedom to read what you like, freedom to have whatever religion you like or lack of religion.

But all that freedom exists in the West today, and yet you were just saying a moment ago that fanaticism has never been so great at any other period.

Well, I don't think it's true that it exists. I mean, take, for instance, what they did in America, which was to go through all public libraries and any book that gave any information about Russia was destroyed. You can't call that exactly tolerant.

WYATT

If we're not enthusiastic we can't get things done. If we're overenthusiastic we run into the danger of being fanatical. How can we be certain that we're doing the right thing and not getting ourselves into a fanatical state?

RUSSELL

Certainty is not ascertainable, but what you can do, I think, is this. You can make it a principle that you will only act upon what you think is probably true. If it will be disastrous if you are mistaken then it is better to withhold action. I should apply that, for instance, to burning people at the stake. I think if the received theology of the ages of persecution had been completely true it would have been a good act to burn heretics at the stake. But if there's the slightest little chance that it's not true then you're doing a bad thing. I think that's the sort of principle on which you've got to go.

WYATT

Would this apply to political parties and governments?

RUSSELL

Oh, certainly it would. I mean, everybody who belongs to a political party thinks the other party's in the wrong; but he wouldn't say that we have a right to go and assassinate them.

WYATT

What are the limits of toleration, and when does toleration turn into license and chaos?

148

RUSSELL

I think the ordinary liberal answer would be that there should be complete toleration as regards the advocacy of opinions as to what the law ought to be; but there should not be complete toleration for advocacy of acts which remain criminal until the law is changed. To take an illustration, you might, for instance, be in favour of reintroducing capital punishment in a country where it doesn't exist, but you shouldn't be free yourself to assassinate somebody that you thought deserved it.

WYATT

Do you think that fanaticism sweeps the world in waves? That it just happens that we are in a wave of it now which will die down in due course?

RUSSELL

Well, they do die down if the surface gets right, but they only die down when the world is in a fairly stable condition. As long as it is in a very unstable condition you have conditions which foster fanaticism, so that I think you have got to try to establish some sort of stability in the world.

WYATT

Do you think there's any chance of reducing fanaticism in the world?

RUSSELL

Oh, I think there's a great chance. I think it depends upon politics. I think that if we had a system where the danger of world war was not a very great one there would be a very rapid growth of toleration and reasonableness both in the East and in the West. But I think as long as this tension exists it is very difficult.

12.
The H-Bomb

12.

WOODROW WYATT

Lord Russell, what do you think will happen if there is an H-bomb war?

LORD RUSSELL

That's an extremely difficult question and I shouldn't like to put the thing to the test of experience, but it seems quite likely that if there was a first-class H-bomb war, practically everybody in the Northern Hemisphere would be exterminated, and a very fair number of people in the Southern Hemisphere would die from fallout. I think it would be a situation in which absolutely nobody would get anything that anybody could possibly want, and it would be a dead end to almost everything that we care about.

WYATT

You mean that it would be a war in which neither side would get a victory?

RUSSELL

Yes. There would be no victories on either side, unless you have a new definition of victory. I mean, it might be, perhaps, that at the end of the war there would be six people left in the Western camp, four people left in Russia, and four people left in China. They then would have a majority of two on their side. Of course, if you thought that a victory you could, but it wouldn't be a very nice one.

Do you think it's likely that there will be an H-bomb war?

I profoundly hope there won't, but I think there is quite a possibility of an H-bomb war as long as things remain as they are now. Chiefly because the need for instant retaliation, which is, from a military point of view, a very real need, means that you're exposed to the risk of some complete misunderstanding, perhaps of a natural phenomenon. One side thinks that the other has begun the H-bomb war, and lets loose the whole thing though nobody really intended it. That is not by any means an impossibility.

Sometimes people say that if you get into a situation in which there is an arms race, this inevitably leads to war. Do you think this so or not?

Well, I shouldn't like to say inevitably—I never like to use the word "inevitably"—but it has as a rule led to war. Most of the arms races that I can think of in history have ended in war. I think psychologically it's very natural they should because the other side's armament causes fear and hatred and leads to greater armament on the one side, and that leads to greater armament again on the other side, and so on. It piles up and piles up and people's nerves get more and more tensed until at last they can't bear the tension, and they think anything's better than this. That is what happens with arms races. It happened before 1914.

WYATT

Don't you think, though that in 1951 when the West began their great rearmament programmes this might have had the effect of stopping a war because it made the Russians feel they couldn't get a quick and easy victory, and so therefore they wouldn't try it.

RUSSELL

It may be so, possibly. It's very difficult to know what was in the minds of the Soviet Government at that time, and one can't be at all sure whether they would have started an aggressive war or not. But in any case I should say that unless something other than the continued arms race is undertaken by governments, it only postpones a war. After all, before 1914 there were crises very similar to the crisis that we've had in the policy of brinkmanship, and those crises didn't lead to war until 1914, and people thought, "Oh, well, if we keep the armaments equal on the two sides, there won't be war." But it wasn't so, and I'm afraid that may happen again.

WYATT

Do you think that there's something to be said for the H-bomb in the sense that the existence of it has made all statesmen and governments so appalled by what would happen if there were a war, they have refrained from having one—even in circumstances such as the various crises over Berlin—when previously they might have started one?

RUSSELL

You can say that and you can maintain it, but I think that, again, history is against you. Everybody remembers that Nobel, who invented the Nobel peace prize and was a very keen advocate of peace, was also the inventor of dynamite. He thought dynamite made war so horrible that there never would be another war. Well, it didn't work out that way, and I'm afraid it may be the same with the H-bomb.

WYATT

Surely the H-bomb is a weapon of an entirely different character. It's not just a larger weapon in the same field, but something which makes it an entirely different sort of instrument.

RUSSELL

Yes, but people get used to things so frightfully quickly. When the atomic bomb was dropped at Hiroshima and Nagasaki the world was struck with terror, and they thought, "How very dreadful this is." Well, now the atomic bomb is counted as a tactical weapon and nobody cares a button about it. It's a nice little old thing like bows and arrows.

WYATT

What are your current views on what it is practically possible to do about the H-bomb?

RUSSELL

Well, there are several things. The first and most easy thing to do is to stop the tests. That would help immediately. In the first place, it would stop fallout which turns out to be much worse than all the experts said it was, an ominous fact. But that isn't quite so important, I think, as the fact that the stopping of tests would prevent the spread of the H-bomb to a lot of new powers. At present as things stand a great many powers both in the East and the Western block are going to get H-bombs, and the chance of an irresponsible government doing something very foolish with them is immensely increased by that; and also the difficulty of getting them abolished is immensely increased. So that I think you should have first of all an agreement to stop the tests, which is quite practical politics and is being considered; and, second, an agreement that new powers should not acquire the H-bomb. If it were a condition of such an agreement that Britain should abandon its H-bomb, I think we should be wise to enter into such an agreement.

WYATT

How are you going to arrive at this agreement and so stop France and other countries with similiar industrial capacity from ever making H-bombs.

RUSSELL

Well, you could only do it, I think, by an agreement between Russia and America that each of them would use all its economic power and all its propaganda power to persuade the satellite nations to follow that policy.

WYATT

Are you suggesting, then, that Britain should have unilateral disarmament in respect to the H-bomb?

RUSSELL

Well, only if it were the condition for such an agreement. If it were a condition for an agreement that only America and Russia should have the bomb, then I think certainly Britain should say: "All right, we'll join in with all the other minor powers."

WYATT

You mean that Britain should really offer to make a bargain by which if she gives up the H-bomb then all these other countries will agree not to make them, and that America and Russia will see to it they won't.

RUSSELL

Yes, I think that would be wise. It's only a first step. It doesn't secure the results that we want to secure, but it would be a first step.

WYATT

Don't you think it would be rather dangerous still to leave just America and Russia with the H-bomb?

RUSSELL

Yes, certainly it would be dangerous, and in fact I don't think you can avoid the danger until you have some quite new political arrangements. Even if nobody had the H-bomb, the knowledge of how to make it exists, and if war broke out it would be made by both sides immediately. So I don't think you can destroy that danger until you have some way of avoiding war, but I think that the likelihood of war would be very much diminished if only those two had the H-bomb. It would diminish the risk of accidental

158

war. It would diminish the risk of some rather madcap government thinking that it would get some good out of starting a war. And altogether it would increase the facility for negotiations with a view to establishing something more stable.

WYATT

Are we now leaving the realm of what it is practically possible to persuade statesmen and governments to do, and entering the realm of what really would be ideal if they would do?

RUSSELL

Not quite yet. I think we'll soon enter that realm, but I think that there is a thing which is quite practicable and immensely important. It is that both sides in the East-West tension should realize that it's important to reach agreements. Hitherto, since 1945, each side has thought the thing is not to reach agreements but to put forward proposals which the other side will have to reject and will take odium for rejecting, and naturally enough that has not led to any agreements. If you get the governments to realize that it's important to reach agreements and not merely to negotiate, you will have made an enormous step forward. This is quite within the realm of practical politics.

WYATT

Surely the real point about the H-bomb, though, is that you've got to avoid wars altogether, because once you have a war then people would start using H-bombs, or start making them even though they'd previously renounced them.

RUSSELL

That is so and for that reason agreements not to make nuclear weapons are not so important as some people think. Their chief importance is that they diminish the tension and make it more possible to reach some kind of permanent arrangement. But the fact is that with the world as it is now and taking account not only of nuclear weapons but of biological and chemical weapons, which may become quite as bad as the H-bomb is—taking account of all those things, the human race will not survive very long unless we find a way of making sure that wars do not occur.

WYATT

Now what do you think that way is?

RUSSELL

There's only one way that I can see and that is the establishment of a world government with a monopoly of all the important weapons of war. A world government whose business it should be to take account of all conflicts between different states; to propose a solution and if necessary enforce that solution; and having such strength that it would be quite useless for any rebel state to attempt to act against it.

WYATT

What armies, navies, and air forces would you leave to the various national governments?

RUSSELL

I should leave only enough for internal order. Just enough for what you might call police action to ensure that the government could enforce its will internally within the country, but not enough to attack anybody else.

WYATT

You mean that Russia, America, and Britain would only be able to put down insurrection internally and not deal with situations, say, in Rhodesia or in some other territory which wasn't strictly their own.

RUSSELL

Yes, I do mean that. The international authority, and not the national state, would have to deal with Rhodesia or whatever it might be. National states all have their own bias. They run up against the contrary bias of other national states, and questions of that sort ought to be settled by an international authority, not by some one powerful nation.

WYATT

Would you contemplate the international authority actually using nuclear weapons against some national state who has refused to obey the findings of an international authority?

RUSSELL

That's an extremely difficult question, to which I shouldn't like to express a definite opinion. I think if it were absolutely necessary one might say yes, but the difficulty about nuclear weapons is that they damage not only the country against which they are directed but all the countries of the world without exception. It makes them quite unlike all previous weapons.

WYATT

Are you optimistic that people and governments will do the right thing about the H-bomb?

RUSSELL

Well, there are times when I'm optimistic and times when I'm not. I don't think anybody can tell how much sense governments will have. One hopes, of course, that in time they will begin to understand the problems they deal with.

13.
The Possible Future of Mankind

13.

WOODROW WYATT

Lord Russell, we've covered a great variety of topics in these talks. What do you think it all amounts to in terms of the hopes and fears of mankind?

LORD RUSSELL

Well, that's an extremely difficult question. I see future possibilities—gloomy ones and hopeful ones—but I think for purposes of definition we had better support gloom.

WYATT

Well, let's start with the gloomy ones. What are the hopes for that, do you think?

RUSSELL

I think—assuming, as we are doing, that the human race does not wipe itself out in a great war—I think the greatest danger that I see is regimentation. I think it's quite possible that under the influence of scientific discoveries and administrative possibilities and organization, the world may get so organized that there will be no fun to be had anywhere.

WYATT

Do you think that the administrative type may become uppermost?

RUSSELL

I think it may. The administrative type combined with a certain kind of scientific efficiency; because the administrative type can do things now that it never could do before. Some of them are good, but a good many of them are not.

WYATT

What sort of things do you think he might do, this administrative type, which might be bad?

RUSSELL

Well, in the first place he could, beginning in infant schools and going onward, get quite enormous power over people's opinions and thoughts, so that what a man thinks, what a man hopes, and what a man fears is determined for him by the education authorities. He will hope and fear exactly as they think he should, and it will be an essential part of such an education that he will be taught to think well of the government, which is not always wise.

WYATT

But won't there always be a strong, independently minded body of people like yourself, who'll be able to disregard this type of teaching?

RUSSELL

I don't think so. No. I mean people of the type I belong to grew up in an old-fashioned world. A more haphazard world than the one that I'm contemplating for the future. The world where there were more loopholes, more exceptions, and where people were not all put into one exact mould, as I can see them being in the future.

166

WYATT

You mentioned something about people not being able to have a personal life if this administrative type got the upper hand. Can you be a little more precise?

RUSSELL

Well, yes. Take what is perhaps an extremely important aspect of this whole thing—take eugenics. Supposing that a scientific government got obsessed with the possibilities of breeding what they thought would be a better race than ours is. It would become fairly obvious from a purely scientific point of view that the future race ought to be bred from, say, five per cent of the males and, say, thirty per cent of the females, and that in order to make sure of this the rest should be sterilized. Well, I think that would be very unpleasant indeed. But I can quite see it happening.

WYATT

But do you think that there really is a serious possibility that science may so obsess people's minds that this sort of thing may happen?

RUSSELL

Yes, I think they might do it in the interests of victory in war, because it's quite clear that you could produce a race that way. Such a race would be far more efficient in war than a people produced by accidental haphazard methods. I think that you could easily persuade people that just as we have thought atomic weapons necessary because the other side was sure to have them, so scientific breeding is necessary because the other side will be sure to do it.

WYATT

All that's a *1984* or *Brave New World* concept. But do you think it applies really outside the communist world? I mean, for example, as far as conformist opinion and so on goes?

RUSSELL

I think it's a little less dangerous in the West than it is in the communist world, but it very, very emphatically exists in the West. Very emphatically.

WYATT

What conformist opinion and conformist dress, habits, and thought, and so on do you think exist?

RUSSELL

Well, take art. I have noticed over and over again when I've been travelling, especially in America, that they have an enormous respect for art, and honour European artists and pay them large numbers of dollars; but no American child is allowed to have the kind of exceptional mentality which is necessary if he is to become an artist. So that all the artists they revere are European and not American.

WYATT

Do you think that art has suffered in Russia?

RUSSELL

Oh—well, I don't know, because I haven't been there, but I should gather so, certainly. In spite of *Doctor Zhivago,* it seems to me that literature certainly has suffered there greatly. I mean, in the czarist time Russian literature was quite supreme and I don't think anybody would say it is now.

What about ballet in Russia?

The ballet is a survival of the czarist time. It seemed to me, when I saw the ballet in 1920, that it produced the impression upon me of cut flowers in a vase. I felt it was very beautiful and very delightful, but hadn't got any fresh vitality from the soil. I think it is now purely a museum piece.

Do you mean you think that all this might lead to a general ossification in which nothing new happens?

Yes. I think there's a very great danger of that. A kind of Byzantine static society that can go on generation after generation much the same until at last it gets so stereotyped that people can't bear it and so sweep it away from boredom.

One of the difficulties that seems to face man is that he can never do anything by halves. He may start off something quite well, and then he takes it to an extreme. Do you think that he'll ever learn moderation?

Well, I'm sure I hope he will. I . . . I think it's very necessary indeed, and I think there is quite a possibility of it.

169

I don't take these gloomy prognostications we have been going through as being gospel truth. I very much hope they won't come off.

WYATT

Can we turn now to the more cheerful things?

RUSSELL

Well, I should say that the first thing that is needed is a realization that the evils of the world, including the evils which formerly could not possibly have been prevented, can now be prevented. They continue to exist only because people have passions in their souls which are evil and which make them unwilling to take the steps to make other people happy. I think the whole trouble in the modern world, given the powers of modern technique, lies in the individual psychology, in the individual person's bad passions. If that were realized, and if it were realized further that to be happy in a modern, closely integrated world you have to put up with your neighbour also being happy, however much you may hate him. . . . I think if those things were realized you could get a world far happier than any that has ever existed before.

WYATT

What sort of evil things do you think you could push away if your people direct their passions in the sort of way you're suggesting?

RUSSELL

Well, first of all war. Second, poverty. In the old days poverty was unavoidable for the majority of the population. Nowadays it isn't. If the world chose it could, within forty years, abolish poverty. Illness of course has been enormously diminished and could be diminished still further. There is no reason why people should be unable to have periods of sheer enjoyment frequently.

WYATT

Well, we're now talking really about the creation of positive good, I suppose. And what other positive good can be produced by man, do you think, in the future?

RUSSELL

I think a great deal depends on education. I think in education you will have to stress that mankind is one family with common interests. That therefore co-operation is more important than competition, and that to love your neighbour is not only a moral duty nominally inculcated by the churches, but is also much the wisest policy from the point of view of your own happiness.

WYATT

One of the benefits that science appears to be about to bring to mankind is that within a comparatively short time the working week will be about ten hours. Now what is man going to do with all this leisure?

RUSSELL

Well, he'll do—if the sort of world that I imagine when I'm feeling happy can exist—he will do what well-to-do, cultivated people have done in the past. Consider, for instance, the eighteenth-century aristocrat, who quite often was a very cultivated man. He had a great deal of leisure and he knew what to do with his leisure, although many of them did things they'd better not have done. Quite a lot of them did very good things, encouraging art, and making beautiful parks and beautiful houses, and altogether things that are desirable. And I foresee when I'm feeling cheerful a world in which that sort of use of leisure will be possible for everybody, because everybody will have reached a sufficient level of culture.

WYATT

What about adventure in this particular field?

RUSSELL

Adventure ought to be arranged for by the authorities. That is to say, the authorities ought to make it possible, without a new expenditure either of money or of time, to provide kinds of really adventurous, and if necessary, dangerous enterprises that vigorous young people enjoy. You ought to be able to go to the poles. You ought to be able to climb high mountains. And if space travel comes along, you ought to be able to indulge in space travel. Things of that sort ought to be provided, and that would channel off the impulses which at present go largely into war.

WYATT

What final message would you like to give to future mankind?

RUSSELL

I should like to say you have, through your knowledge, powers which man never had before. You can use these powers well or you can use them ill. You will use them well if you realize that mankind is all one family and that we can all be happy or we can all be miserable. The time is passed when you could have a happy minority living upon the misery of the great mass. That time is passed. People won't acquiesce in it and you will have to learn to put up with the knowledge that your neighbour is also happy, if you want to be happy yourself. I think if people are wisely educated they will have a more expansive nature and will find no difficulty in allowing the happiness of others as a necessary condition for their own. Sometimes in a vision I see a world of happy human beings, all vigorous, all intelligent, none of them oppressing, none of them oppressed. A world of human beings aware that their common interests outweigh those in which they compete, striving towards those really splendid possibilities that the human intellect and the human imagination make possible. Such a world as I was speaking of can exist if men choose that it should. And if it does exist—if it does come to exist—we shall have a world very much more glorious, very much more splendid, more happy, more full of imagination and of happy emotions than any world that the world has ever known before.

ABOUT THE AUTHOR

Bertrand Arthur William Russell, 3rd Earl Russell, was born in England in 1872. Educated at home by private tutors and then at Trinity College, Cambridge, he has devoted his life to the pursuit of scientific, philosophic, and moral truth. In 1918, in fact, Bertrand Russell served a prison term for writing pacifist propaganda, an experience which he found "in many ways quite agreeable" and which did not prevent him from writing his *Introduction to Mathematical Philosophy* while imprisoned. As a professor, he has lectured widely, having taught at Harvard, the University of Peking, the University of Chicago, and the University of California, as well as at Cambridge where he is a Fellow of Trinity College. He has written more than forty books, including *A History of Western Philosophy, Marriage and Morals, Common Sense and Nuclear Warfare, My Philosophical Development,* and—with Alfred North Whitehead—the monumental work, *Principia Mathematica.*

The grandson of Lord John Russell, the statesman who was the champion of the Parliamentary Reform Bill in 1832 and who, as Foreign Secretary, was partly responsible for maintaining Britain's neutrality during the American Civil War, Bertrand Russell succeeded to the family earldom in 1931. Among the many honors Lord Russell has received as the result of his dedication to "the examined life" are the Order of Merit, bestowed upon him by King George VI in 1949, and the Nobel Prize for literature in 1950. Lord Russell lives at Penrhyndeudraeth, Wales.

THIS BOOK WAS SET IN

BASKERVILLE AND GOUDY OPEN TYPES,

PRINTED, AND BOUND BY

THE HADDON CRAFTSMEN

TYPOGRAPHY AND DESIGN ARE BY

LARRY KAMP

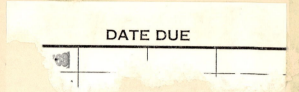

DATE DUE